For Tom -
See you at
the track -
Englehart

Trackrat

MEMOIR OF A FAN

Bob Englehart

Photos by Mark Englehart

Title: Trackrat

ISBN-13: 978-1491065402
ISBN-10: 1491065400
LCCN 2014901308

CreateSpace
North Charleston, South Carolina,
United States of America

For Pat, for every reason

Contents

Acknowledgments

This book would not have been possible without the cooperation, time, interviews and access that the drivers, crewmembers, owners, family members and professionals generously gave me. Thank you all.

Special thanks to Shawn Courchesne, racing writer extraordinaire for the Hartford Courant and RaceDay.com and Scott Running at Stafford Motor Speedway.

Thank you to freelance editor and writer Kathleen White who edited my copy, designer Amy Berman who designed the cover, designer Robin Ohrt for her magic with InDesign, and to photographer Mark Englehart, my son, who took the brilliant pictures not only for this book but also for my article about racing in Hartford Magazine where some of these pictures appeared.

Thank you to Hannah Perlstein Marcus (Sidonia's Thread: The Secrets of a Mother and Daughter Sewing a New Life in America) for her advice and sharing of her CreateSpace experience. Thank you to New York Times best selling author John Lescroart (The Ophelia Cut, The Hunter, et al) for encouraging and inspiring me as a writer, and my friends and colleagues at The Hartford Courant who taught me to write by their talented example.

Witness—April 6, 2008

Winged Midgets line up on the backstretch to be push-started for their 25-lap feature. Take an open-wheeled racecar the size of a bathtub, drop a souped-up, 350-horse-power motor in it, and hang on. The driver sits straight up—no two-way radio, no spotter, no reclining, the steering wheel at the same angle as on a city bus. The seat grips the torso like King Kong's powerful hand. The wing presses the car to the track with such down force, the driver doesn't need to touch the brake going into the corners. The cars take two three-wide parade laps to warm up and return to double-file formation. Coming out of turn four, green-green-green, Erica Santos vaults through the pack. She passes her brother Bobby on the first lap, opening space, diving low, going high, a 10,000-rpm scream past the flag stand. She starts fourth and is in front in only two laps. The woman sitting next to me says it's too cold to race Midgets, that those small tires like it better when it's warmer.

It's early April, and the trees are still bare. The threat of rain hangs in the air with the exhaust from 200 racecars competing in eight different divisions. Spring doesn't grab hold in southern New England until early May, but the racing season started right on schedule at Thompson International Speedway with the aptly named Icebreaker. Spectators are bundled up in heavy blankets and coats, vapor coming out of their mouths like cigarette smoke. Thirty cars on the track are racing into the corners at 148 miles per hour; three laps in less than a minute on this 5/8-mile circuit. Out of the corner of my eye, I see an odd movement back in the pack in turn three. A flying car in midair slams head-on into the red Budweiser sign with a loud bang. It's wedged there, not moving. Jesus, what? Red flag. The drivers coast to a stop and shut off their motors. Smoke and steam waft up from the car stuck in the grotesquely twisted sign. I don't believe what I'm seeing.

The racecar is half-buried in the red sign on the right side about 5 feet above the concrete wall. I can see only the back hump of it, the wing bent at a bizarre angle. The sign is a large soft banner, but heavy steel stanchions support it on both sides.

A racecar stuck in a sign selling beer. I feel an empty, afraid-of-heights hole in my stomach. My heart is sinking, falling into a bottomless pit. "This is a bad one," I say to nobody in particular. I call my wife, Pat, and tell her what I just saw, but it's a short conversation—my voice quavers, my hand shakes. "This is a bad one." I've been an editorial cartoonist for more than 40 years at different newspapers, and when shocking news happens, my instinct is to mentally explore every possibility. I imagine the worst. I imagine the best. I can make myself crazy in a matter of seconds without any help, but this happened right in front of me. I feel sick.

The crowd is quiet. Everyone stands and watches as an ambulance, a fire truck, two state police cruisers, four wreckers, and track safety crews hustle to the scene. I ask a couple of spectators if anybody saw it. How'd it happen? They shrug. Nobody had seen it—we were all watching Erica in the 44 car. By the time I focused on the accident, the flying car was in midair, and I still wasn't sure what I had seen.

"Who is it?" asks a man in a Chevy cap. We can't see the number on the wing because it's mangled and bent. The track announcer says it's Shane Hammond, 27 years old, from Halifax, Massachusetts. How had this happened? I saw Shane's car flying; why was it flying? I look for a witness. I work for a newspaper; facts can help me calm down. I finally find a man who saw Hammond's left front wheel get into the right rear wheel of another car and cartwheel over the wall into the sign. This happens often in open-wheel racing but rarely to this extreme. The man didn't know if Shane had hit the wall first and gone over or if he had missed the wall and hit the sign head on.

Nobody around me has binoculars, so we depend on updates from the track announcers on the PA system and track personnel working with the media. They deliver information as they hear it from the safety crew. The track announcer's electronic voice begins a narrative: "He wasn't thrown. ... There was a brief fire, but the fire fighters sprayed it with foam. ... The cars run on methanol that burns with an invisible flame. ... He's in the car. ... He was driving another racer's back-up car. ... His own car had mechanical trouble earlier in the day. ... They'll take him to Putnam Hospital. ... He comes from a small family. ... His grandfather is Jack Glockner, who used to race Modifieds. ... He has a fiancée. ... The safety crew will take him out of the car. ... His brother, grandfather, and mother will be with him in the ambulance. ... With the new federal privacy laws, we can't tell you anything unless the family gives us permission. ... He's suffering from multiple severe injuries. ... They'll fly him by helicopter to UMass Memorial. ..."

As the safety crew works, the woman next to me sits in a prayerful attitude, eyes closed, hands folded on her lap. I try to quiet my brain and say a silent prayer myself.

I thought back to my anticipation of the new racing season. It started in late winter with two events, a meet and greet at a Harley-Davidson dealership in Ellington and a trade show, Speedway Expo, at the Big East fairgrounds in Massachusetts.

I had talked Pat into going with me to help research a story I was planning to write about racing. "Sure," she said. It reminded her of her Peace Corps cousin; he liked to be dropped into the middle of a cornfield in a strange country where he didn't know the language and had to figure it all out. Pat would go with me to the racetrack maybe once or twice a year, but she's a Long Island girl with an attitude to match. She follows the Yankees and the Jets. Cars are for transportation. When we were dating and went to a race together the first time, we were about to sit in our bleacher seats when a car spun into the wall in front of us. "Sump'n broke," I said. She laughed nervously at my instant transformation into a redneck. "What's so funny?" I asked. "The way you said it." "Racetrack talk," I told her.

The dealership's ad in the paper said some of the top drivers from Stafford Motor Speedway would be signing autographs. In all the years I'd been going to the races, I'd never met a driver at any local track. I'd drawn comic book pictures of racecars and drivers—men I'd made up out of pure imagination, inspired by movies and magazine pictures, but I'd never so much as made eye contact with a driver at the track. I was too much in awe, and besides, I'm an introvert, an observer, too removed to stop a driver striding down the midway with friends, the top of the fire suit loosened, hanging down around the waist, the T-shirt typically advertising motor oil, an engine builder, or a parts distributor. The drivers were in charge, the center of the universe, brave daredevils, poised and confident. I might stare, trying to identify them, but I never stuck out my hand or introduced myself. Maybe it was the fire suit, the knight's armor best admired from a distance, or maybe I was too timid. Anyway, what do you say to people who are willing to risk their lives for my cheap summertime thrills? I built plastic racecars as a kid and went to the track almost every Saturday night with my family, but I never ventured beyond the grandstands, even as an adult.

The parking lot at the Harley dealership was filled with pickup trucks, all American made. My Honda was the only foreign car in the lot, although I like to point out that Americans in Marysville, Ohio, built it. I found a space at the end of the last row and parked in the shade of a shiny black Ford F350 dually.

The dealership sponsored a number of cars in different divisions, so there was a good turnout. Seventeen drivers sat at a long table, all men, ranging in age from the early 20s to maybe 40. They weren't taller, more handsome, more homely, or different in any way from the men walking around the nearest Home Depot. Dressed in jeans and sweatshirts, they looked like anybody. A couple of those anybodies didn't look as though they could squeeze their bellies through the driver's-side window.

Some drivers had stacks of custom postcards for autographs. The ones who didn't signed their sponsors' bumper stickers or track brochures. The postcards were sophisticated, with pictures of the drivers' cars and lists of their accomplishments. The drivers came from every division at the track—Modified, Modified Light, Late Model, Limited Late Model, and Dare Stocks. It was a long table, so I started at the beginning. I wasn't sure what to do. I'd never asked a driver for an autograph, though I had met Richard Petty once in the parking lot at ESPN. Pat and I had just pulled in to our parking space when another car pulled in next to us, and "the King" himself emerged with his entourage. Tall, black mustache, black cowboy hat, black sunglasses, standing there, looking down at me, my reflection in his cool shades. I was stunned. He whipped out a couple of postcards and signed them without being asked. I recovered enough to thank him and ask if he wanted to race to the exit.

I got off to a good start at the head of the table with Todd Owen, a name I recognized from the track and newspaper accounts, last year's Modified champion. He blushed a bit when I asked a question. He said he worked for a construction company when he wasn't racing. I asked about his car, and he told me he had built it from scratch. He explained that there are three ways to get a racecar: buy it used, buy it new, or build it from scratch. I asked him if he raced it more carefully than he would if he had bought it used. The driver next to him made a joke I didn't hear, but Todd said he raced to win. I asked him if I could come visit his race shop someday. To my surprise, he agreed.

I worked my way down the table, meeting more drivers. Some I'd heard of but most I hadn't. Woody Pitkat and the Foster brothers—Scott Jr. and Sean—seemed always to be in victory lane. Woody had short, spiked hair with blond highlights. He and Scott Jr. were cordial and polite, but Sean was downright friendly, a charmer with a well-developed sense of curiosity. He asked me about my editorial cartoons, my politics, where I got my ideas, and my nearly 30 years at the *Hartford Courant* and told me his girlfriend lived in my town. Her father, Don King, owned a touring NASCAR Modified team. We talked about our favorite restaurants and found we both liked the same places.

I continued down the line and got to the end, where a fresh-faced little blond kid sat. Well, he wasn't little—he was

16—but he still had that baby fat and a mouthful of braces. Dillon Moltz had the most sophisticated autograph card of all the drivers, with plenty of graphics and statistics. He said he had driven only half the season last year because his birthday is in June, and the minimum driving age at Stafford is 16. Still, he won a Late Model feature, the youngest driver in the history of the speedway to checker in the division. When I was 16, I was wrestling with the usually stuck gearshift of an oil-leaking, 1950, six-cylinder, four-door Chevy Deluxe. My car wouldn't have gone faster than 80 miles an hour if I had pushed it off a cliff. This kid drove a racecar.

Two weeks after the meet and greet, I went to Speedway Expo. I'd been to many car shows, but this was my first devoted to short track racing. Every space in the exhibition hall was filled with shiny, clean racecars. Most would never look that good again. Tracks, teams, suppliers, driving schools, racing newspapers, magazines, and manufacturers throughout the Northeast were represented. There were seminars: "Media Relations: Grabbing Headlines," "Tires: Why They Do What They Do," "Sponsorship: Finding Corporate Partners for Short Track Race Teams," and "Understanding the Fundamentals of Weight Transfer." Those sounded interesting enough, but the one I was most curious about was "The Fastest Women in the Northeast." How could this not be fun? Women are so much easier to talk with anyway.

On the panel were Renee Dupuis, mid-30s, Nordic features, blond, relaxed; Erica Santos—the woman in the lead when Shane Hammond crashed—early 20s, maybe 5 foot 6 with long, light brown hair falling below her shoulders; and a very short Shelly Perry, also somewhere in her 20s. They welcomed questions from the audience and talked about their careers on the track. Shelly, in her sweet voice, claimed to be 5 foot 1. Maybe in high heels. It was impossible to imagine her climbing through the driver's window.

I pictured a crewmember giving her a leg up as if she were mounting a horse. Maybe it was because of her height, her long, dark brown hair, or her big dimples, but it wasn't hard to imagine how she had looked as a 10-year-old.

Shelly was the 2006 track champion at Stafford Motor Speedway in Modified Lights, an open-wheel, entry-level class. She won the title with a broken wrist from an early-season wreck. She started her racing career as her father's spotter, learning as she went. She wanted in on the fun and began racing Mini Stocks. "I wrecked the car two out of the first three weeks I raced."

Her father raced Modifieds, a cousin raced Late Models, another raced Modifieds in a different division, still another cousin raced karts, and an uncle raced Sportsmen.

Shelly's day job was in human resources at Electric Boat, and she was working on a bachelor's degree in human resources management. She admitted that working on race-cars was like having a full-time job on the side. Her favorite moment at the track is when the announcer says her name, and people applaud. She likes everything about racing, especially the family aspect. "We're so close because we're always together." And she loves the speed. "These cars are wicked cool."

Erica Santos has a bachelor's degree from the University of Massachusetts and is a registered nurse in the Medical Intensive Care Unit at Massachusetts General in Boston. She has a trim build and the caring look of a nurse. She was the first woman to win a feature race in Northeast Midget Association history. Erica and her younger brother, Bobby Santos III, started racing Quarter Midgets at Thompson International Speedway's small track, Little T, when she was 8 years old. Their family traveled all over the country racing. When she was in college, Erica raced in a handful of winged Midget shows. I asked her how she drove on the highway, and she said, "Too fast. I have too many speeding tickets." When she's not racing her car, she works on her brother's Modified team as a spotter and crewmember.

Erica talked about her car again and said the wing makes it harder to drive but that she had a new Esslinger motor and more horsepower. The worst accident she'd been in was when she broke her arm in a Quarter Midget race as a kid; as an adult, she'd had some stitches from a wreck at Stafford. She's raced Modifieds and a 350 Supermodified at speedways in New Hampshire but said Midgets are the most fun. She likes open-wheel cars and said the only danger she saw with winged Midgets was different speeds. "The fastest cars are much faster than the slowest cars." Unmarried, she dates Modified driver Woody Pitkat.

Renee Dupuis graduated with honors from the University of Connecticut, also is single, and was named after Modified driver Rene Charland. He was known as "the French barbecue" for an accident that happened on a track back in the day. He hit the wall, his car caught fire, and fellow driver Ed Flemke Sr. pulled him out of the flaming wreckage. Charland, of course, profusely thanked Flemke, who said, "You'd have done the same for me." Charland said, "Don't be so sure."

***

The air at Thompson is colder now, barely 40 degrees, on-and-off drizzle, the sky the color of faded asphalt. It has taken close to an hour to get Shane Hammond out of his mangled racecar. The ambulance drives slowly through the infield and out the pit gate—no flashing lights, no siren. This is not a good sign. Safety people are cutting away the tangled steel to free Shane's car.

More updates come in over the next half hour and stop

as I keep imagining the family in the emergency room with the broken young driver. I see clumps of fire-fighting foam lightly floating up from the crash site like small, puffy, white clouds. The Northeast Midget Association people announce they're canceling the rest of their race. I see a reporter friend and ask if he knows what's going on. He tells me quietly that

Shane Hammond at Waterford Speedbowl in 2007.
(Deb Marvuglio photo)

his sources in the state police said Shane Hammond had been killed instantly.

I'd never seen a fatal accident at a racetrack, much less a bizarre one like this. I'd seen Dale Earnhardt die at Daytona in 2001 through the filter of television and had seen the grainy black-and-white film footage of Bill Vukovich's fatal Indy wreck in 1955 and Eddie Sach's flaming accident there in 1964. I'd seen photos, read stories, and talked to eyewitnesses, but I had never seen anything like this in person. I'd dispatched many a driver with my pencils and watercolors when I was a boy dreaming about driving at Indy, but it was never me dying, mind you. I always won.

This is what it's like in reality, to see a driver die in a race. It happens so quickly. Even when your eyes focus, you can't believe what you're seeing, what you've just seen. Snap your fingers; it's over, and the damage is assessed. Most of the time, these Midgets flip end over end, sending pieces flying off, spraying broken parts, shedding metal skin, coming to a rest upside down. There's movement in the cockpit, and the driver crawls out and raises a hand—I'm all right. At other times, with bigger, heavier cars and bad luck, the car simply drives head on into the wall and stops. Little damage to the car, but the driver is killed. This is what happened to Dale. On TV, it didn't look that bad.

It's been more than an hour since the race was stopped. I ask which driver Shane got into, but nobody saw. The wounded sign stands twisted, the right stanchion slightly bent. The wreck is cleaned up now; the show must go on. The next division on the track is the Late Models, I guess. I don't know. I wasn't listening. Pro Stocks? Who won? I'm still thinking about Shane Hammond. Twenty-seven. The announcers say he'd been outstanding in karts as a kid. Ironically, he had just won a NEMA award named for the last driver killed in a Midget race 40 years ago. Irony rules in racing. Todd Owen is on the track in a Late Model. Maybe he saw what happened. Drivers are fans too. Maybe he was in the pit stands and saw it all. The crowd slowly returns to a subdued normal. When we saw Dale Earnhardt die at Daytona, we heard months of analysis from NASCAR people about what had happened, but today, we have to process this young driver's death alone. Everyone struggles with his or her thoughts. What do we do with this empty feeling? We're all together but, oddly, individually isolated in this communal experience.

I never met Shane Hammond. What would I be doing right now if I had? What if he had been a friend? Would I be crying now? I feel like it, but strangers surround me. I wish my wife were here so I could cry.

The Whelen 150 is next; 37 touring Modified ground pounders are on the track. The wooden stands vibrate as they go by. There are maybe five wrecks and yellow flags, but I'm not counting. I'm hoping nobody else dies this day; I'm hoping nobody dies in a racecar again—ever.

Many of the spectators here today saw the Blewett brothers' Modified wreck that killed John Blewett III less than a year earlier. Turn one, horrifying irony, brother on brother, the older one who taught the younger one how to drive a racecar. It happened so fast, and eyewitness accounts vary. John and his younger brother Jimmy were fighting for the same real estate for a win: checkers or wreckers. They tangled in turn one, and Jimmy's car went airborne—it happens so quickly—on to the top of John's car. Jimmy's front nerf bumper broke, slicing through the thin sheet-metal top of John's car. The broken bumper found the one vulnerable spot and pierced John's helmet visor, killing him instantly. Snap your fingers; he's gone. I'd read about it in the newspaper. The irony was so powerful that I wanted to write a book about it, and so I had begun my research.

In racing, people die. That's part of the thrill, as primitive and insensitive as that may sound. When people talk about daredevils and death-defying feats of skill, this is what they mean. It's not PR bullshit. It's an unpleasant fact in racing: someone will eventually die.

But people don't go to races to see someone die. They like to see exciting racing, rubbin' and bumpin', tradin' paint, spins, dive-bombing, a pinch into the wall, their favorite driver win. Yes, they like to see a few spectacular wrecks, those people who've never owned a racecar, those people who don't know the effort and money that goes into building one of these machines. But after a wreck, they like to see the driver drop the net and crawl out the window, maybe shake a fist or throw a helmet at the car that caused it. Drivers compartmentalize their emotions so they can do what they have to do to win races, and fans have to compartmentalize too if they want to remain fans after seeing a heart-breaking accident. Even so, I still feel that bottomless pit in my gut. I call my wife again to tell her what happened, what I found out, how I'm feeling. She says I sound as if I'm in shock.

I leave Thompson early, before the 150-lap Modified tour feature is over. Rain is threatening again; I'm cold and shivering, and it has nothing to do with the weather.

The newspapers and racing blogs announce Shane Hammond's death the next day. The winner of the rain-shortened Modified tour race was Ed Flemke Jr., Modified car builder and son of the French barbecue rescuer.

"I'm getting tired of it," Flemke told the *Hartford Courant*. "I'm getting real tired of it. It's just so sad that the price is so great. You hit a foul ball, what's the price? You fumble, what's the price? You fumble the ball here—the price is just too great. I'm just getting tired of it. It's sad, it's really sad. But my dad told me a long time ago to pick that chin up, it's OK to cry, just pick your chin up and you'll be all right. We've got to do it for them. We'll be back. We're too stupid to stop, so we'll be back."

There's a picture of Shane on the NEMA website, smiling brightly, a wide face, wide smile, wide-set Paul McCartney eyes, short brown hair with product in it, a handsome man, a man of his time. Pete Falconi, the NEMA announcer, wrote a sweet obituary calling Shane "a racer's racer. He could turn the wrenches and was admired for his mechanical abilities. He was good on the track too." In his story in the *Courant*, Shawn Courchesne wrote that Shane had made contact with Chris Leonard and gone over the wall. *The Boston Globe* coverage said Shane had survived a brain tumor in childhood but didn't go into more detail about what kind or how old he was when he had it.

Later in the week at Shane's funeral, his best friend and fellow winged Midget driver Randy Cabral considered giving up racing, but when he thought of what his friend would want, he changed his mind. He said that Shane wouldn't have wanted him to give up something he loves. If the tables were turned—if Randy were killed—he'd want Shane to keep racing.

I was there when Shane crashed. I saw them extricate him, and I saw the ambulance take him away. I saw them cut his mangled car out of the sign's stanchion, put it on the back of a flatbed truck, and tie a blue tarp over it to discourage gawkers. I saw the truck slowly drive into the back paddock where the NEMA pits were. I'll forever be a part of it. Shane Hammond died entertaining me. Do I have survivor guilt? I don't know. I'm not a shrink. I do know that I'm left to make sense of it.

A week later, I think of these things as I drive Connecticut's narrow, twisting, unfamiliar back roads. I'm looking for Todd Owen's race shop, but I can't find it because of a charming, quaint, rural Connecticut custom—no signage. I'm lost in the middle of nowhere, in a part of northern Connecticut I know nothing about other than it's the home of one of the state's maximum-security prisons. There're no filling stations, no grocery stores, no convenience stores, and no people to ask for directions. Farms. That's it. With the open fields and patches of snow on the ground lingering in the shadows, it feels like another state. Indiana.

Todd Owen

Connecticut is Manhattan's Land of Milk and Honey, the place you move when your million-dollar, TARP-funded bonus comes through. When New Yorkers think of Connecticut, they don't think of farms or racecars. They think of Fairfield County, Greenwich, private country clubs, insurance companies, WASPy stockbrokers, UConn basketball, a crooked governor, and crooked mayors. I'm driving around lost. I don't know what road I'm on or which direction I'm heading. I call Todd and find out I've driven past his house three times.

Todd Owen lives in a modest ranch house on a large piece of land. His race shop behind is twice the size of the house. This is where it starts and ends, the inner sanctum, the heart and, if not the soul, the center of racing, the shop. My eyes adjust from the cold bright sun to the warm fluorescent-lit interior. Todd Owen is maybe 5 foot 8 in thick-soled sneakers and wears a sweatshirt, jeans, and a worn gray cap.

Todd bought this property from his grandparents. The metal barn holds four racecars—three Modifieds in various states of assembly and a Super Late Model tucked under a tarpaulin. The floor is clean, shiny, and grease free; in fact, the whole garage is downright tidy, organized, a place for everything and everything in its place. No calendars with girly pictures, no racist printouts about President Obama tacked to the wall, no spilled oil or grease anywhere. It doesn't look anything like *my* mechanic's garage.

Todd is rebuilding his number 90 Modified. Its light

Todd Owen

gray, powder-coated tube frame sits on jack stands with no wheels or motor, a rocket sled in the making. Little brass and steel clekos—temporary rivets—hold together unpainted sheet metal panels on the side. This is the car Todd built from scratch, bending the frame pieces around a wooden jig to fit the specifications for the division.

A shelf high above the floor at the far end of the shop

spans the width of the building. The 50 or 60 glistening trophies are arranged with the tallest ones at the ends—some must be 4 feet—and the shortest ones in the middle. Plaques and framed citations cover the wall underneath. A collection of autographed checkered flags hangs above the trophies. The centerpiece of it all is a giant copy of Todd's 2003 Stafford Motor Speedway rookie-of-the-year check for $700. The following year, he came in second in points and has been a top competitor ever since.

Todd, early 30s, medium build, boyish face, blushes slightly when he talks to a stranger. He started racing at 16 at a local track now closed. His dad sponsored a Modified team, and Todd started driving entry-level Street Stocks, working his way up to Pro Stocks and then to Modifieds. A shop that sells motorsport parts and equipment owns his car, and the construction company he works for sponsors him. He rebuilds his car before every season, explaining that most racers buy a kit—frame, body panels, and so on—but he builds his from the ground up. The wooden jig he used to bend the frame is at the car owner's shop. Racing starts at Stafford in a couple of weeks, and Todd's a little behind schedule, but he expects to be ready for the green flag. Three plastic white chairs, the kind popular with Walmart shoppers and suburban dads who use the garage as a man cave rec room, are arranged in front of a big black-and-red pit box, as though someone had been telling a story and then everyone had disappeared in an instant. A collection of Late Model hoods hangs high on the walls; spare nerf bars are below them.

Todd shows me how he uses the large red brake press—as big as an upright piano—to form the side panels from thin sheet metal. The roof is from a 1992 Pontiac Sunbird, the only stock body panel on the car. Even the abbreviated hood is handmade, but he's thinking of buying a pre-formed fiberglass one to make things a little easier. The cockpit and roll cage are reinforced with extra tubing, and the spoiler on the trunk lid is made of transparent Lexan so he can see who's behind him in the race. He points to the front clip—the assembly that holds the front wheels, shocks, and steering—and tells me it's a secret design, so no pictures please.

When he's done bending and fitting the sheet metal, he takes the panels apart and sends them to a body shop run by a friend, who spray paints them a metallic royal blue. Then they're reassembled and fitted with decals for the numbers and sponsors. The motor's installed, along with the wiring, instruments, tires, and everything else that makes an SK Modified.

Stafford Motor Speedway owner Jack Arute Sr. invented the SK division in the late 1970s with advice from driver Ed Flemke Sr. The cost of Modified racing was going through the roof, and car counts were falling. There were few limits on Modifieds, and it was quickly becoming about which owner had the most money. Jack wanted rules that would keep Modified racing affordable, so he and Ed hashed out a plan in Jack's kitchen. Jack's wife came up with the name SK, which stands for nothing. They just liked the way it sounded, like some of the Beatle's lyrics that make no sense. I am the walrus. Goo goo g' joob. It would be interesting to know what a typical 1970s Modified would cost to run today. "I spent $14,000 last year on tires alone," Todd says in his quiet, soft-spoken way. He appreciates the attempt to keep racing costs down and plans to race as long as he can afford it. "But," he adds, "you can't live in a racecar."

Todd calls himself a clean racer. "I'll give up a spot to make sure we finish instead of trying to be a hero. If I can't pass you, I won't push you out of the way." He attributes his success to no fear on the track. Even when he was a punk newbie racing at 16, he says, the older, more experienced drivers on the track didn't intimidate him. "I just wanted to finish. They didn't give you much respect." He won a feature in his first year. "At 16, I was running with the top guys." Sure, it's easy when you're young and bulletproof, no complications, no regrets, just move the sumbitch in front of you out of the way. That's how he drove then. Now at 32, he admits he sees life differently. "I respect the situation more than I used to."

His dad died young—he was 42—when Todd was 19. He says what he likes about racing is "That's the only place I can go in my life and not think of anything else." Todd thinks about his sister Kim. A black-and-red hood hangs on the wall as a memorial to her. The hand-painted inscription reads "Kim Owen, In Our Hearts Forever" with her birth and death years. She was an important part of his team: the statistician, in charge of timing, provider of food and encouragement. She was his family and his friend. She died of a broken neck three years ago at the age of 35 after falling down the stairs taking a load of laundry to the basement.

I'm not going to ask Todd about Shane Hammond's death, not today. A person can die in a number of ways—a fall while carrying a load of laundry down the stairs, a heart attack at 42, or a wreck on the racetrack. NEMA put up a memorial on its website honoring Shane. Thompson International Speedway posted a memorial too.

I'm not going to ask Todd if he ever thinks about dying in a race either. Maybe these deaths are all too fresh for me, for him, for both of us. Instead, I ask him when he gets excited at the track. "When I put my seat belt on." What drains him on the track? "Sitting in the car waiting."

I've always thought racecar drivers were a little bit crazy, like the circus guy shot out of a cannon or Evel Knievel. Todd Owen doesn't seem crazy. Quiet and melancholy, yes. There's a heavy sadness about him. He's still suffering from the death of his sister, and he tells me his girlfriend moved out over the weekend. He understands about his girlfriend. When he's not working, he spends all his time in his race shop or on the track. No time for romantic dinners, long walks in the park, or Friday night dancing, movies, comedy clubs. Friday night is race night—Thursday and Saturday nights too. Sunday is spent bending the car back into shape and digging broken piston rods out of the oil pan.

Before I leave, I look around one more time. A familiar hood hangs on the wall, black with a big red-and-white number 3 on it. I was a Dale Earnhardt fan too. Dale was controversial, sure, but he mostly kept his mouth shut, never whined, and drove with a gunslinger's take-no-prisoners style. When he complained, it was mostly about restrictor plate racing. He wanted to go faster.

Fantasy 500

Skip Barber was a Sports Car Club of America Formula Ford champion and Formula 1 driver back in the 1970s. When he retired, he started his racing school and the Skip Barber Series, a kind of farm system. The class I was in was for rank beginners, but a driver who had the talent, several years, and millions of dollars could go all the way to a Formula 1 ride.

Lime Rock Park, where actor Paul Newman was a regular racer even into his 80s, is nestled in the verdant Litchfield County hills of northwestern Connecticut and surrounded by quaint New England villages, the country playground for wealthy New Yorkers and Hollywood celebrities. I didn't get much sleep the night before the class. I was too excited. All I could think of was what if I couldn't do it, what if I wrecked—that old devil rising, fear of failure. When I was young, I had created a cartoon character, a racecar driver named Eddie Doyle. Eddie Doyle could do it; he never failed.

***

I was 6 years old, tired all the time, and short of breath. I missed school frequently with a sore throat, and my joints hurt, particularly my knees. My concerned mother made an appointment with a pediatrician our family doctor recommended. The doctor's office was in a building downtown. Downtown Fort Wayne, Indiana, was like a foreign country to me, like maybe China. I'd heard of China. I didn't know where it was or what it looked like, but I knew it was foreign. Children who were starving there would appreciate my mother's cooking, according to her. The sidewalks in downtown Fort Wayne were jammed with shoppers carrying bags and briefcases, adults who were so very tall, the men and women all wearing hats. I was wearing a hat too, my little gray cap. Nobody even remotely civilized went downtown without a hat, not even little kids. There were Sears and Roebuck, Woolworth's, Grants, Sheray's Furniture—stores I'd heard of only because of their jingles on the radio.

A spider web of overhead electric trolley wires crisscrossed the intersections. Every now and then, one of the trolley bus's connecting poles slipped off a wire. The driver had to stop, walk outside to the rear of the bus, and maneuver it back on to the wire, a bright spark flash on contact, glowing embers falling to the street. The largest department store in the city was downtown. Wolf and Dessauer covered an entire city block and was central to Fort Wayne's mercantile life. W & D's fashion ads dominated both the morning and evening newspapers, the *Journal-Gazette* and the *News-Sentinel*. Every Christmas, the store put up a four-story-tall, bright neon Santa Claus that covered the entire side of the building, casting a red glow for blocks. The jolly old elf sat in his sleigh filled with presents, cracking his whip over his reindeer. The Christmas season didn't start for my family until we drove to that sign. We'd park our car on the street, the motor running, the heater fan purring, and stare out the windows like tourists.

I knew nothing then of synagogues or mosques, but all the major Christian religions in the city—Methodist, Lutheran, Presbyterian, Episcopal, and Catholic—had Gothic cathedrals downtown. Around the corner from the Catholic cathedral was the Mizpah Shrine Temple Auditorium, home to the Shrine Circus, touring big band acts, and Broadway road shows. The Lincoln Bank—once the tallest building in Indiana, where my father worked as a teller—sat across the street from the Allen County Courthouse, a gray granite building that looked to me like the United States Capitol in Washington, D.C. The courthouse's claim to fame was that Charles Lindbergh had once flown over it. There was energy downtown, the exotic, mysterious, frightening energy of unfamiliarity. I knew my neighbors on McKinnie Avenue, but the people downtown—where did they come from? There were black people downtown. There were no black people in my neighborhood. My pediatrician's office was on the second floor of an old brick building. The waiting room smelled of rubbing alcohol and had white-painted walls with dark wood trim and large windows that looked out over the street below. That would be the last time I saw the doctor in his office. The next time would be in my bedroom.

He told me I had rheumatic fever. I had no idea what that meant; I heard it as romantic fever. He told me I was going to have to stay in bed and rest. I couldn't walk, run, ride my bike, or play with my friends. He told me I had to keep my heart rested, that what I had—this romantic fever—was a deadly disease that could kill me. He explained it in a way a 6-year-old boy could understand. "Your heart is like a fort full of brave soldiers that's surrounded by Indians. Every time you get out of bed and walk or run or ride your bike, the Indians creep closer to the fort. If you don't stay in bed and rest, the Indians will overrun the fort and kill all the soldiers, and you'll die."

No ambiguity there—not that I knew what ambiguity was. I was too young to be afraid; fear and terror would come later. How long do I have to stay in bed? "Six months," said the doctor. As it turned out, it was a year. The only time I left that bed was to go to the bathroom—my mother carried me—and go to the doctor's office twice a month so a nurse could draw blood. I was not a good patient in that regard; I whined and cried. One time, a particularly incompetent nurse stuck me several times trying to find a vein, and I had a screaming fit. My mother, a high-strung woman not given to yelling at anyone other than family, grabbed my arm away from the nurse, loudly called her a butcher, and took me home. We went back a couple of days later. We never saw that nurse again.

Penicillin was the only treatment for rheumatic fever then. It came in a bottle as a thick, chalky, pink liquid sludge I had to force down my throat every day. Sometimes my mother and I fought about it, and it made me gag. I still can't abide a certain shade of pink. It makes me want to vomit. All day long, sitting in bed every day, I drew pictures. When I wasn't drawing, I read my brightly illustrated children's books.

My father had built our small house on McKinnie Avenue after World War II with help from friends. It had two bedrooms and a screened-in front porch, the whole place covered with white fiber cement siding—probably loaded with asbestos. We had a one-car detached garage in back, also painted white, with three maple trees and my sandbox behind it. Everything inside the house was a different shade of beige. I think my mother found the color soothing, and my father didn't care one way or the other. In the living room were a couch, two chairs, a hassock, a floor lamp, a small desk with a radio on it, and my mother's sewing machine.

When the taxman came to the house to assess personal property, my mother moved the sewing machine into the closet. When I got older, I helped her.

The basement was my private club, my playground. A big oil gravity furnace sat in the middle like a sheet metal octopus, round duct pipes spreading out in every direction. A large old nicked and scratched dining room table sat against one wall, a hand-me-down from my grandparents. The oil tank sat in one corner, and at the foot of the stairs were a washer and dryer. One day, the load in the washer became unbalanced, and the vibration caused the machine to walk across the floor until it reached the end of the electric cord and stopped. I saw it happen and was sure the washing machine was alive. I never quite trusted it after that. After my diagnosis, my parents moved my brother Tim—who was a year old and still in a crib—into their bedroom, and my mother set up a folding card table—beige—next to my bed. There was plenty of room for my watercolor paints, paper, pencils, crayons, and brushes.

That room became my world; the white cotton chenille bedspread with rows of little tufts reminded me of a farm field of cabbage. I would heap it into mountains, valleys, and passes just right for staging ambushes on my plastic cowboys, Indians, and soldiers. The walls were soft fiberboard that dented easily, and under a window was a small desk I wouldn't sit at for a long time. It was a corner room. The window above the desk looked out over the backyard, and another one faced our neighbor's driveway. I lived every day in my blue-and-green striped pajamas; my only escape was on paper.

When my father brought home an unused roll of adding machine tape from the bank, I drew freight trains hundreds of cars long. While I painted, I listened to the radio—we had no television then. Few people did. In warm months, I heard the sounds of my friends playing outside, yelling, squealing, and laughing. I could identify them by their voices. I wasn't supposed to get out of bed, but sometimes I would go to the window and look. There was nobody there; the voices were coming from down the street. How I yearned to be out there with them. During the school year, a tutor visited once a week so I could keep up with my class. Once, a photographer from the *Journal-Gazette* came to take my picture, and a reporter wrote about the new program the school system offered for homebound children with long-term illnesses such as rheumatic fever and polio.

Friends of my aunt and uncle owned the Rialto, our neighborhood movie theater, and we went often before I got sick. I loved Westerns, war movies, and the newsreels. That's where I saw highlights from the Indianapolis 500 for the first time. I'd never been to a live auto race, but it grabbed my attention on the big screen. Bill Vukovich fascinated me; he seemed to always be in the winner's circle. I liked his smile, and he was popular with pretty girls, so I decided I wanted to be a racecar driver. There were two short tracks in Fort Wayne, but my parents weren't fans. I wouldn't discover the fun of live speedway racing until later.

When I wasn't drawing cowboys, Indians, and racecars, I drew circuses. I'd been to the circus only once, when I was 5, and it scared me. I was afraid of loud noises, such as firecrackers and popping balloons. Even the sound of a cap gun made me put my hands over my ears. The clowns used loud firecrackers in their routines and as scary as they were from a distance, those clowns were terrifying up close. I was in the hallway with my mother at the Mizpah Shrine Temple Auditorium. The Shrine Circus was in town, and my mother had gotten two tickets. We were filing in to see the show, and a clown was in the hallway, mingling with the customers and their children. I was trying to disappear inside my mother's fur coat so the clown wouldn't see me, but it was too late. He turned, bent low, and said, "Hello, little boy." I don't know if it was the voice suddenly coming out of that painted white face or the fact that it was a raspy, cigarette-roasted growl, but I burst out crying and watched the entire show with my fingers in my ears.

Although I was afraid of clowns, I wasn't afraid of my disease. The doctor had explained that I had some control over it. I could beat the Indians if I followed his orders. I could conquer my fears by drawing them.

On Memorial Day in 1952, I was listening to the Indy 500 on the radio, which then was run only on the official holiday, even if it fell on a Wednesday. The fastest car in the time trials barely broke 135 miles an hour, so the race lasted most of the afternoon at those speeds. Drawing furiously, I made up my own racecar drivers based on the men I'd seen in the newsreels and pictures in the papers and magazines. I even provided my own sound effects, which were fairly convincing. Bill Vukovich led for most of the race, but all of a sudden, he was out. He pulled over on the track with mechanical trouble. That's when Eddie Doyle was born.

Troy Ruttman takes the lead coming out of turn one, but wait! Coming up fast behind him is the number 7 car, Eddie Doyle. Doyle and Ruttman are wheel to wheel. Doyle drops behind Ruttman and dives to the inside in turn three. Doyle takes the lead! There's traffic ahead. Wait! The screech of tires—a car hits the wall in turn four! Crash! A fire! Doyle drives through the burning gasoline and takes the checkered flag to win the Indianapolis 500!

My mother opened the door. "Are you OK?" she asked. I looked up from my drawing board.

"Yes, why?"

"I thought I heard screaming."

"Those were tires," I told her. Eddie Doyle. I'm not sure where I got the name, probably from seeing a picture in a

magazine of the 1940 winning car, the Boyle Special. Eddie Doyle drove at Indy, and he was as real in my imagination as any driver on tour. I gave him the number 7, my lucky number, the day I was born. He was strong, handsome, brave, and single. He won every race, and when he wasn't racing, he spent his time kissing pretty girls. He drove a Kurtis-Kraft roadster with an Offenhauser motor, and he wrecked it often. One time, his left foot was mangled badly in a flaming accident that left him with a slight limp for the rest of his life. He joked about it, saying he was lucky it was his brake pedal foot because he didn't use it that much. For a whole long year, my world was my small bedroom, but almost every day, I went to the circus, made a long railroad train, rode the range, or raced at Indianapolis.

Finally, the doctor said the rheumatic fever was gone, the soldiers had saved the fort, and I could go outside and play.

I was supposed to take it easy, though—no running and no riding my bike for a while. The first time I walked out the front door, the summer day was warm and sunny, and the front sidewalk stretched toward freedom, to downtown, to everywhere. As soon as I got out of sight of the house, I ran like the wind. I jumped up and down and ran some more. I rode my friend's bike down the sidewalk as fast as I could. I pushed my friends in the wagon, climbed the apple tree down the block, played catch, played baseball in the empty lot. In short, I was a normal 7-year-old. For the rest of my childhood, though, if I became bored or angry with whatever my friends were doing outside, I'd go home to draw pictures in my bedroom. My mother would stick her head in. "You feel OK?" she'd ask. I'd tell her that I was feeling fine. I just wanted to draw.

When I was sent to my room for punishment, I'd draw pictures and create all the sound effects and voices for each character in my adventure. My mother would tiptoe down the hallway and suddenly open my door. "I wanted to see if you were alone. I thought you had somebody in here."

Cowboys, Indians, and circuses faded away, but Eddie Doyle stayed and grew. My bike became a racecar; so did my wagon. The living room floor was the Indianapolis Motor Speedway. My parents finally bought a TV in 1953, just before the only station in town signed on, and one of the first movies we watched was *The Big Wheel*, starring Mickey Rooney as a hotheaded Midget driver. Eddie Doyle grew from racing Indy to racing everything. I would arrange the cushions on the couch to be my Sprint car, a plastic dinner plate my steering wheel. At other times, the couch was a Ferrari, a Jaguar, a Late Model, or a Midget. I knew nothing of a real racecar driver's life, but I knew it was exciting. It had to be. I made it that way.

***

My Skip Barber class was the first of the day, a pleasantly cool morning just right for racing. We were lucky with the weather. It had rained all week and the night before, but the sun was bright, and steam drifted lazily up off the wet track. There were 13 of us, mostly young—I was clearly the oldest person in the class—and mostly men, but a couple of women were driving too. Some students were driving out of curiosity, another two or three were celebrating birthdays, and one couple was celebrating their wedding anniversary. The class was a little over three hours long, about half that time in the classroom and pre-race preparations and the other half driving on the 1.53-mile road course.

The classroom lesson was about basic racing skills spelled out and diagrammed on a white board: hitting the marks, tire patch, downshifting, acceleration, the line, questions, and what to do should you have an accident. "Don't close your eyes when you wreck," said the instructor. "You'll miss the best part."

I put on the two-tone red-and-black driver's suit and white helmet the school provided and went downstairs to the pits. I don't own driver's gloves or shoes, so I had brought along a pair of winter golf gloves and wore black sneakers. From a distance, I might've looked like I knew what I was doing.

The cars were lined up double file, their streamlined bodies opened like clamshells, exposing the motors and inner workings, the pit crew bent over the machines, making last-minute adjustments. The cars all looked the same: red-and-white Formula Dodges, low to the ground, open wheels, open cockpits, with four-speed transmissions powered by rear-mounted four-cylinder engines capable of 130 miles an hour. The instructor pointed out the shift lever attached to the tubular frame on the right side, the very small brake, and the clutch and throttle pedals.

When I eased into the car, I was lying nearly flat on my back, my rear end 6 inches off the ground. I couldn't see the pedals—the car wrapped around me like a carbon fiber cocoon—so I had to feel for them. The seat was adjustable. The instructor showed me the proper racing position related to the seat and the steering wheel. Stretch your arm forward, keep it straight over the wheel, and lower it. The top of the steering wheel should rest in the crook of your wrist. He helped me adjust my five-point harness, pulled it tight, and showed me how to quick-release it in case I had to get out in a hurry. Hurry? "You mean if it's on fire?" "Don't worry about fire," he said. "In case you have to go to the bathroom." Then he told me to make sure the transmission was in neutral, flip the ignition switch to the on position, and press the red button. The powerful motor vibrated to life, a smart rumble, muffled for the neighbors. I was scared to death.

Then, when I put it into first gear, let out the clutch just a little, and followed the instructor's car—a red, turbocharged, race-ready Dodge Neon SRT4—onto the track, Eddie Doyle took over. All the years of imagining, pretending, driving my passenger cars, my mother's sofa, my model cars, making up adventures with pen and paper were behind the wheel of that racecar. I let out a whoop that I was certain could be heard over the motor. It felt so right. All fear passed. I could've done this, I thought. I could've been a racecar driver, except for one problem. I was a big chicken shit.

The handling was precise, and everything responded instantly: throttle, brakes, steering. I shifted smoothly through the gears as we drove through Big Bend, which is really two corners. Don't over-slow the entry. At the apex, release the brake, add some throttle to settle the rear end, roll over the curbing, look ahead to the Lefthander. Don't worry about the brakes; you'll use TTO—trailing throttle oversteer—to position the car for entry into the turn. Look to the left at the apex; now turn in for the Righthander. Again, look ahead, stay on the throttle, you're coming to No-Name Straight. It's not quite a straight, more of a slight zigzag, but don't lift; drift to the left to enter the Uphill. Gradually pick up speed, faster until we reach the top of the hill—it rises 60 feet—by the chicane. Make sure you're tracked out and the car's straight when you reach the top. Even the slowest cars get light coming over the crest of the hill. Throttle, faster and faster to West Bend's high-speed corner, moderate braking, throttle through the turn, stay up with the instructor, under the Bailey Bridge to the scariest part of the track, a hard right turn at the bottom of a steep hill. I'd been to Lime Rock a couple of times, had seen cars scream through the Downhill at incredible speeds, wondering how the drivers kept the cars on the track. Now it was my turn.

We flew down the hill, a 60-foot drop. We're going too fast, I thought, but I put my faith in my car and the instructor in front of me. At the bottom of the hill, just before the turn, the track flattened out, the compression zone. Gravity pressed down hard. I turned the wheel to the right, downshifted into third, and felt as though I could go through that corner a helluva a lot faster than that. Not even one lap completed, and I was ready to turn pro.

As we shot down the quarter-mile straight to Big Bend again, I watched the markers fly by ... five ... four ... three ... and prepared to downshift. I'd researched heel-and-toe shifting, an impossibly coordinated way of downshifting without losing engine revs. It involves braking with the ball of the right foot while putting the heel on the throttle, punching the gas—a "blip," they call it—while pushing in the clutch with the left foot and shifting into the next lowest gear. I tried it and dropped far behind the instructor's car. The next lap, I decided to try something different. I'd always been pretty good at speed shifting—flooring the accelerator and shifting while the accelerator is wide open by quickly jamming the clutch to the floor and shoving the gearshift into the next highest gear. Do it right, and it's faster than an automatic. Do it wrong, and you're on the street picking up small pieces of the drive shaft.

As we came in to the turn, I hit the clutch, jammed the gearshift into third, and slowed without using the brake. Again, the same thing into second. Each time, it made a hard clunk but went right into gear without losing rpms. What the hell, I thought. Ain't my transmission.

After a few laps, we pitted, and the instructor critiqued our driving. He told me to stay closer to his car. I told him I was giving him a couple of car lengths as I do on the street. "We're not on the street," he said. I asked him how often the school went through transmissions, and he told me they were surprisingly durable. I quit worrying about damaging the car and concentrated on staying right on the instructor's ass. Comedian Jerry Seinfeld had taken the class and wrecked his car. He felt so bad about it that he put a Skip Barber School magnet on the refrigerator in the kitchen set of his TV show.

I had no idea how fast we were going. A racecar doesn't have a speedometer, but the faster we went, the safer I felt. The car was built from the ground up just for racing. The tires, the frame, everything was designed to help me go fast. My adrenaline was driving it now, faster and faster. I aimed for the orange cones, hit my marks, my shifts, rode onto the striped curb, through Big Bend, the Lefthander, the Righthander, No-Name Straight, 60 feet up the steep hill, the front end pointed toward the sky, jamming into fourth gear just before the crest, through West Bend, the Downhill, downshift to third—thank you, gravity—onto the Main Straight, floor it, stay right behind the instructor, into Big Bend again and again.

Going into a turn, I heard tires screech behind me. Out of the corner of my eye, I saw one of the students spin into the grass. I laughed. "Loser," I yelled to myself. I quickly got into the rhythm of the track. I wasn't driving my mother's sofa, wasn't pretending; I was driving a racecar and driving it hard. When we pitted for the last time, I told the instructor, "I could've passed you." I could've too—in my imagination.

Months later, I took a Late Model driving class with a friend at Thompson International Speedway. We'd raced go-karts a couple of times at an indoor track in the winter. I'd already learned something important: a go-kart is harder to drive than a racecar. It was a very hot, humid August afternoon at Thompson. The class started with a basic half-hour instructional meeting in the scorer's box high above the speedway. While the instructor was talking, we heard tires screech and looked out the big glass window to see one of the cars plow into the wall in turn two. "Flat tire," said the instructor. Flat tire?

We filed down to the infield where Late Models were lined up; a rack of helmets sat next to a rack of fire suits. We were the second class of the day, and when I put on my worn-out, powder blue driver's suit, it was damp from somebody else's sweat. I did a Goldilocks search for a helmet. They were either too tight or too loose. When I found one I thought might be just right and put it on, the inside was soaked with cold sweat. I would've tossed it, but it had taken too long to find, what with me being a pinhead. I'm lucky to find a hat that fits, let alone a racing helmet. Next time, I'll bring a head sock, a balaclava, as we sophisticated road racers like to call it. Again, I wore my pair of winter golf gloves and black sneakers.

We had an option to buy a couple of hot laps in a two-seater with a professional racecar driver to get an idea of how fast we should be going. My friend went out first and when he came in, he looked shaken. I asked him if the speed had gotten to him. He said it hadn't been the speed, but he'd had an attack of claustrophobia in the car. I thought that was strange and suggested he drive the Modified sitting over by the pit wall instead of one of the Late Models.

When I went out for my two laps with the driver, I saw what my friend meant. I don't get claustrophobia, but the inside of a Late Model is nothing like I had imagined; visibility is severely limited. Maybe it looks different from the driver's seat, but either way, I was determined. I had paid for these two laps, and I wanted to get my money's worth. I also wanted to see whether the driver drove with two feet or one. The instructor showed us how to climb in to the car through the passenger window. Face front, put your left leg in, park your butt on the sill, straddle the door, tuck your balls out of the way, swing your right leg through the window onto the seat, and lower yourself in.

The instructor helped me with the harness, pulling it tight, and pounded twice on the roof. I asked the driver his name just as he started the motor, so I didn't hear anything but a roaring 350-cubic-inch V-8. He didn't waste any time getting up to speed on the track. By the time we left pit lane, we were in third gear on the backstretch. By turn three—the turn where Shane Hammond had crashed—we were flying.

I had to hang on to the middle cross-member and pull myself toward the driver with all my strength against the lateral G-forces to see what his feet were doing. Two feet: one on the throttle, and one on the brake. This would be a problem. I've been driving all my life with one foot, the way I had been taught in driver's ed. The only time I used my left foot was for the clutch, as at Lime Rock. On the street, a couple days before the class, I had practiced driving with two feet and made such herky-jerky stops that I nearly made myself carsick, and I don't get carsick. When we pulled into the pits after two laps, I had a good idea of how fast I'd have to go to be a real racecar driver, one foot or not.

After driving a nimble Formula Dodge, the big black, white, and red Chevy Late Model I chose felt like a dump truck, with the emphasis on dump. The outside of the car was in average shape, looking like a typical weekend warrior ride, but the inside was a slum. Marbles—the small pieces of tire that come off during a race—littered the floor of the car. The shabby interior looked like dust and rust. The view from the driver's seat didn't look much different than from the passenger's seat, and the driver's seat was not adjustable. The steering wheel was too far away for me to feel comfortable. The cowl was high and the seat—an old design with small bolsters holding my head and body still—was upright but reclined backward slightly. I was going to climb out and pick another car, one that fit better, but everyone in the class was in their chosen ride.

I could see why spotters were so important and my friend had felt claustrophobic. Three straps run down the middle of the windshield. The thickly padded roll cage surrounded me, the bolsters on the side of my head in the driver's seat blocked my side view, the high cowl, the helmet—all I could see was straight ahead. The instructor gave each of us ear buds for our radios so we could hear the race director. I examined them closely before I put them in. The race director gave us some last-minute instructions over the radio about passing only on the right and some other rules, but I wasn't listening. I was thinking about the possibility of touching some stranger's earwax. The spotter checked in; I could hear him, but it was a one-way hookup, so I couldn't talk to him. I would've asked him if they sterilized the ear buds. I flipped the ignition switch and punched the red starter button, and the car roared to life. This was not the powerful buzz of a racing four-banger. This was the throaty, gravelly, T. rex growl of a racing V-8 cursing the stillness of the countryside. Jesus. Can I drive this thing? We filed out onto the track.

I went through the gears, turn three, turn four. When I got to turn one, I was at speed. I lifted going into the corner, and a loud backfire set my ears ringing even through the padding of the helmet and the ear buds. Going faster now, turn two, the back straight into turn three, lift—blam!— that backfire. The faster I went, the louder the explosion. That would be my guide. I would see how loud I could make that bastard pop.

Coming out of turn four, down the front straight. Again, as at Lime Rock, roll into the throttle, keep the tires just this side of spinning, foot down more, more, to the floor now, go in deep, lift—blam!—foot on the brake— yes, the right foot. One-foot wonder. I didn't notice the awkward seat position, the rust, the dust, or the marbles. I was flying, passing my friend and all the other cars once, twice, three times. I had signed up for 15 hot laps. It would be over in minutes. Black flag. What? Me?

I pulled into the pits. "Is your radio working?" asked the instructor. "I don't know; have you been talking to me?" My radio had conked out. They wanted me to slow down. I had racked up 15 laps in a little over five minutes. What can I say? I'm a racecar driver!

After my hot laps were over, an instructor took my picture inside the racecar. While I waited for a printout, I sat in the infield pits talking to one of the students, a man in his late 40s. He was a driver who'd raced several seasons at Thompson but retired because he couldn't afford to be competitive anymore. Once a year, he took the class just to get behind the wheel again. I asked him if he ever thought about dying on the racetrack. He said he thought about dying all the time. The only time he *didn't* think about it was when he was on the track.

I had to admit that both times I'd driven racecars, the fear of dying was the farthest thing from my mind. The only thing I thought about was going faster. I told myself that I was a racecar driver, but racing is more than speed. It's one thing to drive a racecar in a class under closely supervised conditions and another to race with 35 hungry, competitive, experienced drivers for 25 or 40 or 150 laps.

When I got home, I told Pat about my experience and asked if she was interested in taking the class just for the fun of it. I explained to her that she could control her speed, that she didn't have to fly around the track like a maniac—like me—on the edge of control. She said maybe, but only if she could see over the steering wheel.

Carbon-X Fire Retardant Sports Bra

Racing is the only sport in which female athletes are required to wear a Carbon-X fire-retardant sports bra. There aren't that many female racecar drivers, yet there are more women in racing than in any other male-dominated sport. There are no women on my local minor-league baseball and hockey teams, certainly no women on the University of Connecticut football team. The UConn women's basketball team is famously dominant, but the women don't play the men. Racing is the one sport in which physical strength doesn't necessarily determine a winner. It's all in the head. It helps to have a good setup too.

Renee Dupuis's race shop is at the end of a downhill-sloping driveway behind her parents' suburban home not far from my house. Two dark brown horses, still wearing their shaggy winter coats, watch me from a small corral next to the building. Renee greets me at the door with a firm handshake. She's nearly as tall as I am and stands in a relaxed posture, arms folded, sometimes casually leaning against a pit box, at other times leaning against a wall. She speaks in a contralto, maybe a habit formed from competing with men.

She moves and talks easily, her long blond hair flowing casually over her shoulders. We walk past the antique 1932 Plymouth coupe her father is restoring while two Jack Russell terriers bounce around at our feet. Her goateed brother, Jason, is wiring the instrument panel on one of the two identical red-and-yellow Modifieds they race, both sitting fully assembled on lifts. Her trophies are neatly arranged on shelves behind the cars, and the floor is spotless. I have to admit this is not what I expected—Todd Owen's shop and now this one. I check my shoes to make sure they're clean—wouldn't want to be tracking horse crap all over this shiny floor.

Renee and Jason, who is also her crew chief, began racing Quarter Midgets at Silver City in Meriden and Thompson's Little T when they were kids; she was 4. Eventually, she began winning more races than he did and took over the driver's seat. She was the first woman to win a Modified feature race in the history of Riverside Park Speedway. She joined the NASCAR Whelen Modified Tour, the oldest touring division in NASCAR, in 2002 and came in second for rookie of the year. Today, she's a member of Indy driver Lyn St. James's Automotive Team and Project Podium, organizations that broaden public awareness and offer scholarships to women in racing.

The two tour cars in Renee's shop look similar to the local SK Modifieds except everything is more expensive and shinier, the motors' internal parts the best money can buy. I've seen crewmembers in the pits wiping down a tour car with Windex and paper towels. Wreck on Saturday? That car had better be spotless by the next show the following week. The tour has high standards, and the officials don't care what things cost. Well, they care, but not that much, not at the expense of top-of-the-line professionalism.

Renee Dupuis and Jimmy Blewett sign autographs at Stafford Motor Speedway.

Renee likes the complexity of racing. "Every time you're in the car, you forget about work and everything that's going on." She chose Modifieds because her dad, David Dupuis, was a Modified driver at Stafford Motor Speedway. Early in her career, she broke her left foot in a wreck there in turn four. Her car spun and slid, hit the wall, and came to a rest at the start/finish line on fire. When I ask her what she was thinking, she says calmly, "I thought, it's on fire. I probably need to get out." Repairing her foot required three different surgeries.

Renee likes Thompson. "It's more forgiving." She was in the race when John Blewett III died and displays a decal on her car memorializing him. She points to a bar, part of the roll cage behind the driver's seat, called a Danbury bar, or the "brain bar." She says the failure of this caused

John's death. I ask her about Shane Hammond's accident. "I always think that we never should've been racing that day. It was way too cold and throughout our feature, at least, there was a heavy mist falling. I know the accident wasn't weather related but nonetheless." She talks about Dale Earnhardt's death, using the euphemism "passed away." Passed away? He hit a wall head-on at 180 miles an hour. My wife's grandmother "passed away" in her sleep. NASCAR's reactive tradition is to investigate the cause after a fatality and make safety improvements if it can. Earnhardt's death ushered in the HANS device, an acronym that stands for head and neck support. All the Sprint Cup drivers use it, and it's mandatory on the Whelen Tour. Renee doesn't like it because it robs her of visibility, so she relies more than ever on spotters.

I ask her about fear on the track. She says a certain amount of fear is healthy. "It teaches you respect." She is a mechanic, has a good feel for the car, and can identify mechanical problems. "I'm always on the radio saying, 'You're not going to believe this.'"

Renee works for the International Brotherhood of Boilermakers union as an administrator in the apprenticeship program and listens to soft rock in the shop. "I'm sick of country."

Troyer Engineering in Rochester, New York, built her Modified. It's a "roller," meaning it came with the frame, body, suspension, bumpers, and nerf bars. She and her crew spent long hours adding the rest—brakes, seat, suspension, tires, motor, and transmission. The motor alone costs as much as a high-end passenger car—$40,000 to $60,000. She could buy a spec motor for $25,000, but it couldn't be rebuilt and would have to be discarded when it was spent. She says that every cent she has goes into the racecar. It costs $100,000 a year for basic maintenance racing, $150,000 to be competitive. Like Todd Owen's, her crew is made up of friends, family, and volunteers. To raise money, she starts each season with a fund-raiser at a local banquet facility complete with a live band and dancing.

Renee patiently explains the instrument panel. Moving from left to right: the starter button, main ignition switch, another switch to go between two ignition systems, a switch for the radiator fan, switch for the oil fan, oil pressure idiot light, running light, oil pressure gauge, water temperature gauge, red handle for the built-in fire extinguisher, oil temperature gauge, and the red knob of the brake bias adjuster. I ask her why she does this, why she risks her life, why she spends so much money. She says she loves the sensation of speed. At the start of the race when she steps on the gas, "You feel the car grab the racetrack, and it puts your brain back in your head. You might be sick or not feeling well. You always feel a little better when you get to the racetrack."

I ask her if she raced women drivers differently from men. "I'm pretty much always the only girl in all the races I've been in."

Driving home from Renee's shop, I call Erica Santos and catch her in her car on the way to work. She drives a Honda, by the way. "I really want to win races," she says. "I don't care about points. It's all about fun. I'm a very competitive person." She was and still is the only woman to win a NEMA feature race in the history of the organization but doesn't want to be known for winning only one race. If she's racing her favorite tracks, Stafford and Waterford—"There's lots of room at Waterford, lots of passing"—she starts getting excited about it a week before. She and her brother, Bobby III, are another pair of third-generation racers. Her dad, Robert Jr., raced Pro-4's, Pro Stocks, and her grandfather Robert Sr. raced Modifieds. Like Renee, she lives with her parents.

Erica went to Shane's wake and the reception afterward. "We're a club," she says. I've heard it before, that racecar drivers are in a club, a unique group of people who are separate from the rest of the world. I ask her if there is a special tradition involved with the wake of a racecar driver, such as the bottle of whiskey the Hell's Angels like to bury with the deceased or the fire fighter's last ride in a coffin on a fire truck to the cemetery. Erica says there's nothing special, just standing around talking.

I ask how Shane's death affected her. "I don't know," she says. "It's really upsetting. It could've happened to anybody." Would she consider quitting, as Randy Cabral did? She says no. "I wouldn't want anybody else to quit because I died in a wreck," and she changes the subject. "The car is handling really well," she says.

Erica's boyfriend, Woody Pitkat, doesn't like to talk about death on the racetrack either. He's a regular top three in Late Model and Modified races, so he's experienced at talking to the media about racing but not about personal matters. That's another quaint Connecticut custom not limited to racecar drivers. Unlike in the Midwest, people here don't open up about themselves until they get to know you. In Indiana, Illinois, and Ohio, they'll spill their guts to anyone who'll listen at the first meeting. Well, maybe not the first meeting but definitely the second.

Pit Cat

Woody Pitkat is one of the few local drivers making a living entirely from short track racing. When he's not driving, he's the car chief for Don King Racing, a Whelen Modified Tour team. He's a consistent winner and top-ten finisher in Late Model and Modifieds at both speedways. Between his salary at King and the thousand-dollar-plus payouts for his wins, seconds, and thirds at the tracks, he does all right. I call and ask if I can visit him at work in the King race shop. He says sure. I ask him what time. He says anytime.

The headquarters of Don King Racing is on a quiet street in Middletown, Connecticut. King—no relation of or resemblance to the boxing promoter—is one of the few owners who don't ask their drivers to bring a wad of sponsorship money. He finds his own.

The house is a typical suburban two-story colonial up against a forest of old maples and oak trees next to a seldom-used and rusted railroad track. A toter-hauler, a Chevy dually, and a Cadillac sit in a large gravel parking lot between the house and the track. There is no sign of life. I expect the sound of a racecar engine revving or a pit gun whine, but all I hear are the sparrows chirping in the junipers. I wander around the yard trying to determine where the shop is and hear pounding and drilling coming from the two-car garage under the house. I open the side door to bright fluorescents lighting two shiny Modifieds without wheels sitting on jack stands. The cars are identical—both painted metallic wine red and gray, spotless, gleaming in the light. Woody is bent over the motor of one car while two men work on the body of the other. The two men look surprised that I'm there but say nothing. The tall, quiet man with the gray hair and beard casually smoking a cigarette is Don King, owner, crew chief, and former drag racer.

And there's Woody, driver, mechanic, hands-on master of the setup mix of track bars, tires, springs, and shocks that can shave a tenth of a second on a half-mile circuit. Here's a racecar driver built like Eddie Doyle, except for the glasses. Woody, late 20s, 6 feet or taller, his dark eyes showing a friendly intensity, answers questions while he works, but his focus is on the motor. His situation is typical among the top local drivers. At Stafford, he drives an SK Modified owned by Davidson Foods and a Late Model owned by Pat and Marcia Kretschman. At Thompson, he drives a Sunoco Modified, which is nearly the same as an SK, owned by Bob Hitchcock and Kelly Iverson. He helps other local teams, touring groups, and girlfriend Erica Santos's winged Midget crew. Jimmy Civalli drives this King car, but Woody could just as easily.

He says he gets excited at the speedway: "When you're out in back lining up to go on the track, thinking about what you're trying to do or what you want to do." He's inspired to win by his Hitchcock crew chief, Jimmy Fuller, the younger brother of drivers Rick and Jeff. About Jimmy,

Woody says, "He never quits, never backs down. You have to give your all, 100 percent when you work for him. Give it

Woody Pitkat at a drivers' meeting at Stafford Motor Speedway.

the best, go out every night, and think you're going to win." He admits he has some things to work on, such as his temper. "Somebody'd get into the back of me, I'd get mad and spin out on the next lap." He also admitted that he could learn to handle the pressure a little better. "A lot of it is stuff off the track. When you're at the track, you have to weed it out." Talk about stuff off the track: he became a father on Valentine's Day with the birth of his daughter, Ella, to an ex-girlfriend.

Woody keeps moving while he talks, now to the right front shock, then to the innards of the front clip. My goal is to stay out of the way, not slow him down. God knows I don't want to knock something over in this tight space. I can see it now, me knocking a car off the jack stands. So much of my life has been about imagination. Does Woody visualize the race beforehand? "I'll talk to some of the drivers. You can see some of the cars are not as good, but when you think something is going to happen, it's never like that. It doesn't happen the way you think it will. Some nights you're racing, no matter what you do, nothing works. You do the best you can. One night, I won five races in a row. I couldn't do anything wrong. I got the lucky breaks." And how does he shake off a bad night? "It's hard if it's something big, like running out of fuel. I ran out of fuel once in a 150-lap race with eight laps to go. That shouldn't happen." He's driven Midgets only once, and it didn't turn out well. The motor gave him trouble in practice and conked out on him during the race, a rare DNF.

On top of driving three racecars regularly and occasionally a touring stock car, Woody plays hockey in one of the local leagues. "Know anybody looking for a goalie?" This guy likes to stay busy.

Woody grew up in Stafford Springs, home of Stafford Motor Speedway. When he was a kid, his grandmother took him to watch his uncle race in upstate New York. As soon as he turned 16, he got a NASCAR driver's license and started racing at Stafford, first in DARE Stocks in 1996 and then in Late Models and Modifieds. He's won championships at Thompson and Stafford, the most popular driver 11 times at both tracks and rookie of the year at Thompson. I once saw this guy get the lucky dog twice in the same feature race and come back to win it.

I'm starting to notice the uncomfortable silence in the garage. The men are working hard to get both racecars ready for the first Whelen Modified Tour race of the season. There's not a lot of room to get around two cars and a pit box, and I'm clearly in the way. I ask Woody if I can meet him at the shop of the owner he drives for at Thompson. He says that would be fine. I ask him when. He says anytime.

A week later, I drive more than an hour to some little Massachusetts town near the Connecticut border in the boonies, get lost twice, and finally figure out that the gravel road to Hitchcock Pool Water, the home of Black Dog Racing, is basically a narrow dirt lane behind a construction company. The neighborhood looks like a mix of rural, industrial, and residential. I call Woody to tell him I'm on my way, but he's still at Don King Racing in Middletown, working on the car. Now I'm not quite sure what to do, but I figure as long as I'm here, I might as well see if anyone on the team is around.

I park my car in the big gravel lot and search for the door. A dog barks loudly from inside. I go to another door and open it a crack, ready to slam it shut if the dog attacks. There are three men in the back of the garage, one wearing a mechanic's uniform from a Mercedes dealership. I tell them who I am and that I was supposed to meet Woody, but he's still back in Middletown. They laugh and shoot "typical Woody" looks at one another. They tell me the dog—the namesake black dog—won't bite and invite me to stay.

Now this race shop is more like it. This is how I'd imagined it, kind of like a Possum Lodge boys club, a tree house on the ground. There must be a Big Mouth Billy Bass in here somewhere. The walls are scruffy and lined with dusty trophies, the floor is scruffy, even the black dog is scruffy. Two identical glistening black-and-gold number 99 Sunoco Modifieds on jack stands are in better shape than the shop, but as messy as the shop is, this team was second in the national NASCAR All-American series in 2007. Apparently, neatness doesn't count in racing.

Bob Hitchcock owns the cars in partnership with his girlfriend of 22 years, Kelly Iverson. Bob, tall with sandy hair and mustache, looks as if he could've been a cowboy in another life. He introduces boyish-looking crew chief Jimmy Fuller and young mechanic Paul Blackweller, the man in the Mercedes uniform. I ask Jimmy what his day job is, and he says he works at UMass Hospital. I ask him what he does there. "Brain surgeon." Excellent. This is another thing I expect, a smartass, just like me. He relents and says he's in facilities, which I guess means he's a janitor. He's married, has young children, and comes from a racing family—brothers Jeff and Rick are behind the wheel. Paul Blackweller, early 20s, is the team go-to guy. He likes the simplicity of a racecar as compared to a new Mercedes. "Modern passenger cars are full of sensors and computers. Everything's mechanical on a racecar." He started with the team last year. His grandfather was a drag racer in the South. I ask him if he ever drove. "No," he said. "There are more opportunities to work on a racecar than to drive a racecar."

I thought I was a mechanic when I bought my first car, a 1950 dark blue Chevy Deluxe. I bought it used from a real mechanic who worked at the Texaco filling station in the old neighborhood near the drugstore where I hung out with my friends. I had worked as a carryout boy at a grocery, at a car wash, and as a dishwasher at a restaurant and a United Auto Workers cafeteria to save $200. I was 16. I had a beginner's permit, so my mother drove Uncle Dick and me to the filling station to pick up the car. I counted $150 cash out to the mechanic, who seemed to be relieved, and Uncle Dick and I drove home in my first car. It had six cylinders, four doors, and a three-on-the-tree transmission, and I didn't stall it once.

After years of building model cars and reading hot-rod magazines, I didn't waste any time customizing it. I took it to Earl Schieb and had him paint it a lighter metallic blue and put on a set of baby moon hubcaps. I spray painted the dashboard white myself, hung fuzzy dice from the rear-view mirror, put on a chrome gearshift knob, and bought some fancy seat covers for the front and rear seats. I bought two big tires for the rear, flipped the leaf springs for added height, and attached a lowering shackle kit to compress the front springs. The rear end was high and the front low to the ground, giving it what hot-rodders called a California rake. When I cruised through the drive-ins with my friends in the car, the angle was so severe that we'd slide off the front seat.

My first mechanical job was a tune-up—points, plugs, and condenser. Easy enough. I'd heard about it and had seen a mechanic working under the hood of my parents' car once. How hard could it be? I'm a guy, right? Guys just know how to do that stuff. A friend of mine was working part-time at a garage on the other side of town, and we used an empty bay with his boss's blessing.

"You know how to do a tune-up?" asked the boss. "Sure," I said, "how hard can it be?"

"Go ahead," he said. "Knock yourself out."

The first thing I did was to disconnect the spark plug wires from the distributor. Then I disconnected the wires from the spark plugs and lined them up on the workbench. The boss came over.

"You know the firing order on this car?" The what?

"The firing order. You know what I'm talking about?" I told him no.

"The spark plugs don't all fire at once. There's a sequence. Maybe number one cylinder fires, then maybe number four fires, then number three. Who knows? You've taken all the wires off. How you going to put them back on the distributor without knowing the proper sequence? I thought you knew how to do a tune-up." I spent the rest of the day hunting for a repair manual that listed the firing order for the cylinders in a 1950 Chevy Deluxe six-cylinder engine.

I tell this story to the guys at the Hitchcock garage. When I finish, they look at one another—a knowing look—did this guy just step out of a time machine? Rip Van Winkle himself, all long white beard and sleepy-eyed.

"Distributors aren't like that anymore," says Paul. My phone rings; it's Woody. He says he has a lot of work to do and won't be able to make it out to the shop. I ask when we can get together at Hitchcock's. He says anytime.

Foster Brothers

Randy Cabral wins the NEMA feature at the Speedbowl the week after Shane Hammond's wreck and dedicates the victory to Shane. I wasn't there; I read about it in the *Hartford Courant*. I wasn't ready to go back to a racetrack because I didn't want to run the risk of seeing another driver die in a wreck, but two weeks later, I'm at Stafford Motor Speedway looking for answers. I can't stay away from it; I have to know what makes this closed, insular world behind the pit gate tick. It's the Spring Sizzler, Stafford's opening race of the season.

After a week of cold rain, the air has warmed and patches of light blue mottle the gray sky. The tall maple and oak trees behind the back straight spread their bare branches over the noisy idling Modifieds lined up along pit road, but the trees have taken on a slightly pink blush. This is mud season. The fragrant smell of blooming spicebushes mixes with the exhaust fumes, fried dough, French fries, spilled beer, and burned rubber.

I drag Pat along. When I draw Pat's caricature, I give

her a ruby red heart-shaped mouth, big brown eyes, dark eyebrows, and a snow cone of white hair piled high on top of her head. She has advanced powers of observation and can easily see right through complicated situations and people; I've watched her freeze men in their tracks with one look. I never have to worry about her going out alone at night.

Pat cuts a deal with me. She'll go to the races in the afternoon if I'll go to a music recital in the evening. Her piano teacher's high school–aged son is a gifted pianist and violinist and is performing in a small theater at a private school that night. Her first discovery is that there's graffiti about Ted Christopher in the women's room.

Ted Christopher is the 800-pound gorilla in Northeast racing. He's raced everything from Daytona prototypes at the 24-hour endurance race in Florida to Three-Quarter Midgets at an indoor arena in Providence. He's pretty much won everything and not always to the delight of the fans of other drivers. Pat reports that "Ted Christopher sucks" and that "TC is a dirty racer" is the most popular invective. A Danbury trash hauler owned Christopher's car until the end of last season. There was some graffiti suggesting that TC and the trash hauler were engaging in a common homosexual act, but you really can't rely on graffiti to tell the truth. Anyway, I think it's some kind of honor for a male racecar driver to be the subject of graffiti in the women's bathroom.

The paddock at Stafford is acres and acres of gray asphalt marked off with worn white stripes to designate each team's pit stall. The space for each racecar is not much wider than the parking lot space at your local supermarket, but on a bad night, there's enough room for a team to install a new motor before the start of a feature. Parked at the head of each space is a trailer big enough to hold the racecar, pit box, and a few extra tires. Some of the tour teams and the luckier local boys park toter homes and giant haulers in the middle of the paddock. The Dare Stocks usually come in on open trailers towed by any manner of vehicle, the beat-up Ford pickup being the most popular.

The dress code in the paddock forbids open-toed shoes, sandals, or shorts. Makes sense if you think about brushing against a hot exhaust pipe or dropping a lug wrench on your foot. No alcohol either, and I assume the same goes for the usual illegal drugs.

NASCAR sanctions all three short tracks in Connecticut. Stafford is a popular track among drivers and fans, although the drivers complain about all the rules and regulations. "It's run like, well, like NASCAR," said one driver. They run the Friday night show with precision quickly and smoothly from division to division; there's little down time between races. The PA system in the paddock is always haranguing the drivers in the different divisions. "Let's go SKs. Line up for your feature. Dare Stocks line up. Last call for Late Models. Line up."

If Thompson International Speedway is the big brother—brawling, sprawling, deadly fast—and the largest Connecticut track at 5/8 of a mile, the Waterford Speedbowl is the funky high-school dropout little brother always in danger of going out of business. Waterford is Connecticut's smallest track at a third or 3/8 of a mile, depending on how you measure it and whom you're talking to. The 'Bowl has an asphalt-paved paddock behind the back straight, but the paddock behind turns one and two, where touring groups such as NEMA pit, is pea gravel and dirt. Every time a race-car moves, it sends up a choking cloud of dust. The rusty old bent catch fence looks as though it would be right at home on the perimeter of an abandoned junkyard. But drivers love the track—its asphalt surface scarred and pitted like an old boxer's face—and the track has its reliable regulars who've raced there for generations.

Stafford Motor Speedway is the middle brother who went to college: highly professional, tightly run and regulated. In fact, one car owner told me she was racing at Thompson next year. "Too many rules at Stafford," she said. Stafford is the state's oldest track, starting as a horseracing track at the original Stafford Springs fairgrounds 100 years ago. The track is as safe as any track can be, with a catch fence all the way around and a safety zone 20 feet wide separating the spectators from the front straight. A SAFER soft wall is in troublesome turn one, and a metal guard rail about 4 feet high that circles the track can absorb some of the impact when a 2,600-pound car slams into it at 120 miles an hour.

Sean Foster comes in second in the Limited Late Model feature. When he wins, with his crew and sponsors gathered in victory lane, he yells his signature line into the microphone: "Racecar! Racecar! Here we go, racecar!"

I'm quickly finding out that talking to people about death on the track during a race is a waste of time and, let's face it, a downer. The media is focused on what's happening on the track, the fans on having a good time, and the drivers and crews on racing and, more important, winning. After finishing his interview in the press box, Sean comes back to his pit stall with a devilish smile and ready to tease.

"You make up your cartoons or steal them?" he asks.

"I make them up. Do you cheat?"

"What's cheating?" He sounded so innocent, and I didn't know the answer.

I ask if Shane Hammond's death had affected him. Sean's more than 6 feet tall, thin, with short brown hair, a slight underbite, and a mischievously ornery glint in his blue eyes. He peers down at me, says no, and looks at me as though I were nuts, as though dying on the racetrack was the last thing on his mind. I ask him why he races. "For glory, for friends, for family, for bringing everybody together, for excitement, for partying after the races—I got a billion reasons."

"Tell me about the partying after the races.

"Well, last night, my friend got so drunk, he shit his pants."

Sean Foster doesn't look anything like his nickname, "the Grenade." Matt Buckler, the colorful announcer at all three Connecticut speedways, gave it to him while describing one of Scan's racing moves. Buckler is famous for his Dan Rather–like descriptions of what's happening on the track:

Sick Rick is a few gears short of a transmission (about a demolition derby driver.)

He's all over the back bumper like bandages on a mummy.

Sand is good for camel racing but not for cars (when a car spun into the infield dirt).

His tires are like denture cream.

He's all over him like crust on a chicken pie.

He's been around since the invention of asphalt (about a 70-year-old racecar driver).

There's debris on the track. That's French for trash.

The landlord of the outside groove (on a driver's come-from-behind win).

They touched wheels and wound up in daisy country.

Three-wide genocide.

The top three cars could fit inside a cowboy hat.

Sean Foster is a grenade, and he's about to pull the pin.

In the early days of short track racing, a wannabe driver would buy an old coupe with a V-8 motor, soup it up in almost unlimited ways that are now banned, chop off the fenders, weld the doors shut, paint a number on it, and drive it to the track to race. Most of the modern young drivers started organized racing in go-karts or Quarter Midgets when they were kids. Sean and his brother, Scott Jr., are typical. They started racing karts but several years apart. Scott is six years older and about 5 inches shorter than Sean. They never raced against each other in karts because of the age difference; as adults, they race in different Late Model divisions. Sean says that if you figure in karts, Scott Jr. has won more races, but he also says that if he were to race his brother, "I'd race him harder than anybody else out there."

Sean's signature victory cry came from a prank he pulled one early morning at Stafford. Many of the drivers and crew spend weekends camped there. Some drivers come from as

Sean Foster

far away as Pennsylvania, New Jersey, northern Maine, and occasionally from the Midwest. Motor homes, toters, and even a few tents crowd into the enormous back dirt and gravel parking lot. A couple of years ago, after a night of post-race partying, Sean, up at dawn and armed with a bull-horn, went around to the campers where other drivers were sound asleep and yelled, "Racecar! Racecar! Here we go, racecar!" The drivers didn't think it was funny at the time, but the fans in the bleachers love it when he yells it into a microphone in a post-race interview after a win.

Sean's girlfriend, Christie King, blond, attractive, mid-20s, the daughter of Whelen Modified Tour car owner Don King, helps on the Foster team when she's not helping her father's team. Everybody in local short track racing is related somehow, through blood, marriage, or dating. Scott Foster Sr. drove Street Stocks and owns the team, both cars, and the electrical contracting company where his sons work as electricians. The crew is family and friends. Mother Sue is on the team too, measuring tire temperatures and feeding the hungry bunch. She offers Pat and me sandwiches from a tray inside their spacious trailer.

Sean likes to win. "I hate second," he says. He admits that after work, the rest of his life centers on racing. He likes the local scene and has no plans to move on to NASCAR. He has an unusual one-handed driving style, his right hand resting on his right leg and his left hand steering the car. It seems to work for him; he was the 2007 Limited Late Model champion.

The worst wreck he's been in wasn't on the track but this past winter in a snowmobile accident, when he broke his collarbone. He drove today's first race of the season in pain but turned down an operation because it would have side-lined him for weeks. He pulls back the top of his fire suit to show us a permanent bump where his collarbone meets his shoulder.

Sean and Christie met in elementary school when they

were kids, and they met again at the track when they were adults. Christie taught him the proper way to drive a racecar one day when they were returning from her father's beach cottage. She challenged him to follow her all the way home driving with both feet. This afternoon, she's upset that Sean isn't wearing the fireproof underwear she got him for Christmas.

Christie doesn't drive, but she grew up with racing. "It's the only thing my dad and I have in common." She's the statistician for her father's team, keeping track of laps, who got tires, who's pitted, and anything else that can help the spotter and driver. She's an elementary school math teacher during the week.

The wind picks up, and gray clouds are rolling in from the west. Please, God, no rain. Scott Foster Jr. has the pit stall next to his brother. He has a dark brown goatee and mustache and wears a red-and-black fire suit and a faded Boston Red Sox cap. He is married to Jennifer, who's home with their young daughter, Ashley. He didn't do the usual progression up the racing ladder but made a giant leap from racing karts to Late Models when he was 18.

Stafford is a challenge for Scott Jr. "It's a driver's track," he says. "It's a track where experience pays off." He has plenty of experience here, but he learns something new every time. He likes Thompson because of the speed, the high banking, and the upper groove on the edge by the wall. He thinks about it for a moment and says it again, "I love the speed." His favorite track is long closed. Riverside Park was located north of Hartford in Agawam, Massachusetts, in the middle of an amusement park by the same name. It was the first track I visited when I moved to Connecticut, a quarter-mile asphalt bullring with the pits crammed between the back straight and the Connecticut River. Everything was paved asphalt, even the infield. I saw my first figure-eight race there. The

star of the show on most Saturday nights was Reggie Rug-
geiro in his hot Modified.

"It was a fun place to race," says Scott. "Double grooves,
tight competition, you're always in traffic. I never raced there
on a regular basis, just a handful of times in Strictly Stock.
I ran my Late Model for an outlaw race. I ran my SK there
for a special race." His team's motto was "Win or lose, we
still booze. We always went out into the parking lot after the
big race. That was the fun part of Riverside. Everybody went
out into the parking lot. People would fight and be enemies,
and the next thing you know, they're buying you a drink.
Everybody went to the bar across the street." That's where
he met his wife—one of the rare spouses not from a racing
family. She had been there with a girlfriend who went to the
track every week.

Scott's favorite division is Pro Stock, similar to a Late
Model but with a bigger motor and racing on slicks like a
cup car. "In my opinion, it's a real racecar. With Pro Stock,
there are no stock frames. They're beautiful cars, pretty,
lightweight, a lot of horsepower. An SK Modified is an un-
derpowered car." The SK is a big momentum racecar with
massive tires and not a lot of horsepower. It's a different
type of racing. "A lot of slamming, beating, banging. In Pro
Stock, you've got to finesse your way by somebody. You've
got to set somebody up. With SK, you see these guys out
there that will just dive bomb, feed you the nerf bar, and
shove you out of the way. It's a rough type of racing. It never
fit my driving style." Once he was racing an SK and was
slammed from behind so hard that his helmet shifted down
over his eyes. He had to lift it up to see where he was going
but the impact didn't move the car. "I was never on the verge
of losing control."

Scott likes the outlaw-type Super Late Models they race
in the Pro All Star Series (PASS) but says it's out of the Fos-

ters' budget. He guesses it costs $500,000 a year to run a season, but he's not sure. "I know some of those guys are running $50,000 engines."

He loves the competition. Some of his most memorable races were ones he didn't win. "I love being with other good drivers that you can race with. And this is very rare, but sometimes you get in these races when you're with other drivers you trust, that you can run door to door with. You know you're not going to get turned by them, but maybe you can trade a little paint and race that tight race and slice and dice and back and forth. Back and forth racing, that's what I like."

He's a nervous wreck at the track before a race. "All through the day, I'm a bit of a mess, but once I get on the track, I put the helmet on, I'm as calm as can be." The only time he was injured in a race was when he was racing karts. He broke his collarbone—seems to be a weakness in the Foster family—when he flipped upside down. He never thinks about dying in a race. "If you start thinking about stuff like that, you're not going to be any good at it because you can't go out there thinking and worrying about how you're going to get hurt. The safety of these cars has gone so far. A lot has to go wrong to get hurt, but it happens."

Scott calls himself a clean racer. "I'll race you how you race me. If you want to race me clean, I'll race you clean all day long. The minute you start thinking you're going to push me around … nobody's going to push me around on the racetrack."

Eddie Doyle has something to say about that.

I was racing a late model at Baer Field. I'd just come off an Indy tour race and was looking to unwind with a little hardcore fender action. My crew chief, Blackie Felton, owned the car, and he put me in the seat. It wasn't all that fast, and I was kind of doing him a favor, him being a hell of a crew chief and a good friend, but I was having fun.

I was running eighth, and I'm trying to get by this guy in front of me. I wasn't really that fast, and I know I'm not going anywhere, so I'm not going to do anything stupid like wreck the car or wreck somebody else just to pick up seventh when that's as far as I'm going anyway. I looked in the mirror, and this guy was coming up on me pretty quick, so I know he's faster than me. My first thought was to let him go because I figure he's going to try a peek under me, so when he did that, I'd just point him to the inside, you know, just wave out the window and let him go. No sense trying to hold up somebody who's 2/10ths faster than you.

Well, that asshole never tried to make any kind of a racing move on me. He caught me, got into the left rear, and punted me out of the way. There ain't no walls or guard rails in the turns at Baer Field. That bastard almost put me over the side into a cornfield. I figured he was some dumb-ass local boy trying to make a name, you know, take on the big shot Indy driver, his way of saying you ain't so hot. Well, I was pissed. I drove as hard as I had all night long but kind of condensed like, you know, 15 laps worth of hard driving squeezed into the last ten laps. I chased him down, and on the last lap, I was running third and he was second. I got into his ass and sent him to the moon. I got a little sideways, and I think I finished ninth or so. I didn't care. Blackie didn't care either. He knows me. He said the son of a bitch asked for it.

After the race, the guy comes over to our trailer and, oh man, he's really pissed. He was so mad—all red in the face—he kind of made me laugh a little bit. He says, "What the hell was that all about? Are you crazy?" I told him that he'd put the same move on me. I says, let me tell you one thing and don't ever forget this. Nobody, I mean nobody is going to push me around on the racetrack. I will wreck myself just to get you if that's the way you want to race. So the guy started whining and complaining, but by then, I wasn't listening. I knew what I was doing. You've got to stand your ground and, to some extent, make them think you're a little bit crazy. Even if you're bluffing. You make them think you're a nut job, and they'll leave you alone. Well, he stood there kind a quiet for a few seconds. Then he asks me for my autograph.

Scott Jr. is not a NASCAR fan. "It's cookie-cutter boring stuff. NASCAR is worried about their cups and trucks, and they could give a damn about the little guys like us. We're forced to join their organization, and they don't do a thing for us."

What angers Scott most is how the rules have changed over the years, how the local and regional tracks have started looking out for their interests only. He can't race his Stafford Motor Speedway Late Model at any of the other tracks in Connecticut because of the various division regulations imposed by each facility. He wants standardization, and he blames NASCAR for the lack of it. "They let the tracks do anything they want. NASCAR should stand up for us and say if you're a NASCAR sanctioned track, this is what a Late Model is and this is the rules you're going to run. If you went out West and told them that you live within an hour of three different tracks and you could only race one, they'd laugh at you." Scott Jr. looks to the sky as a few light raindrops begin to fall.

"You can't fight city hall."

The rain stops as quickly as it started, only enough to briefly slow the action on the track with a short yellow. Nobody wants to talk about dying on a racetrack, except tour Modified driver Ed Flemke Jr. "I'll talk about anything. I don't care." This is not a good time, though. He's preparing to race in the 200-lap tour feature and the team is preoccupied, but he invites Pat and me to visit his shop later in the week.

Ted Christopher wins the tour feature with a controversial move and surely another line of graffiti in the women's bathroom. I read about the race in the *Courant* the next day because we had to leave early to go home and change into something a little dressier than jeans and T-shirts for the recital.

This is my life now. In the afternoon, I'm sitting in a trailer at Stafford Motor Speedway listening to a racecar driver tell me about his friend who was so drunk at the party the night before, he shit his pants. In the evening, I'm listening to a piano and violin recital by a teenaged prodigy performing Paganini.

Grandstand Honors

Ed Flemke Jr. loves music, the music of a finely tuned racecar engine. His shop may be the nicest one around. It has a comfortable kitchen that would look good in any home, white cabinets, pewter handles and drawer pulls, an espresso maker on the counter, two wine racks on top of the refrigerator filled with good wine, and freshly killed venison in the freezer. We sit at a glass-topped table that has a diorama underneath of an antique toy boat and two tin toy cars, probably collectibles. The black matching chairs are modern and comfortable.

Ed co-owns Race Works with fellow champion driver Reggie Ruggiero. Their company builds Modified racecars for local and tour drivers. They do everything, except the motors and the paint. There are four cars in the big garage in different stages of assembly.

"Business has been good," says Ed. "Yesterday there were seven."

He's 54 years old and single, with brown hair turning gray and a salt-and-pepper mustache. His size makes it easy for him to slip through a driver's window. With his distinguished mustache, he looks more like a banker than a racecar driver. Talking with Ed requires blocking out a minimum of

Ed Flemke Jr.

an hour and a half. He will not only talk your ear off but also may choke up with emotion at any moment with the remembrance of people he has loved and lost, particularly his father, Ed Flemke Sr., a legend in Modified racing. Ed Sr. won more than 500 races in his career and was an innovative setup man and one of racing's best teachers. Ironically, he didn't teach Ed Jr. much at all, but that seemed to be his plan. The father wanted the son to learn on his own. As a result, Ed Jr. raced in his father's shadow for years.

Ed's a thoughtful man with strong opinions. "Racing needs to be pulled back," he says. "It's getting way too expensive. Reggie and I were talking about it just this morning. If we had to start our careers today, we wouldn't make it past Street Stock."

Ed isn't a natural racer, as his dad was. His parents divorced when he was 4, and his mother, who raised him, did everything she could to steer him away from racing. "The legacy of his father was something I worried about," she said in a *Hartford Courant* interview. "For any second-generation driver, it's very difficult. I knew then that the pressure that would be on him to be like his father would not be fair. Nobody could be the driver his father was. There was also a part of me that didn't want to see him get hurt, and, really, it was such a consuming thing. It was that way for his father, all consuming, and I didn't want to see that for my son."

Ed was determined and worked hard at it. His sister was the natural racer. When they were kids, they raced karts around the yard, and she always won. Their father used to tell visitors, "Watch my daughter kick the shit out of my son."

Ed starts to tell his dad's favorite quote but doesn't finish it. "My dad used to say, 'I missed the opportunity to be *born* in a racecar, so. ...'" Ed's eyes well up as he chokes back tears. After a moment, he explains that his father didn't die in a racecar. He died of a massive heart attack in the driveway of his home, slumped over the steering wheel of his snowplow truck. He was 53.

When he was just 16, Ed and a friend bought a Modified. Ed had recently gotten his driver's license and had learned to drive a stick just three days earlier. They hauled it to the track and made the decision right there that one would drive and the other would crew chief. If that didn't work out, they'd switch roles.

Ed didn't know anything about racing. His father took the car out on the track to test it and brought it back into the pits. He got out of the car, strapped Ed in, and said, "OK, go ahead." That was it. That's all he said. Ed took it out onto the track and ran three laps, and his father waved him in. He reached inside the cockpit and said, "OK, this time put it in high gear." Ed knew the shift pattern for a three-speed transmission, but he'd installed the linkage backward, so it shifted backward. He couldn't even tell by the rpms of the motor that it was in the wrong gear. Ed's father watched for a while and told Ed he had to leave for his race at Thompson. His parting words to his son that night: "The only person you have to impress is yourself." Ed had no idea what his dad meant but came to understand that his father was not going to be much help.

Racing has changed since the father watched the son struggle at Riverside. There are a lot more regulations now. NASCAR and other tracks keep changing the rules that in effect make the arena smaller, causing more intense competition. The Blewett brothers' wreck at Thompson had been building for a long time. Ed's worst wreck came at Jennerstown Speedway in Jennerstown, Pennsylvania, when he hit the wall, broke two ribs, and knocked himself unconscious. While he was out, he had a dream, a man's voice telling him he was going back, that he had more work to do. He wasn't going to die.

"These cars aren't dangerous," he says. "What we do with them is dangerous." At any given NASCAR-sanctioned racetrack, the rules cover everything from the fuel cell vent to the color of the driveshaft. The roll cage and frame is a secure enclosure like a shark cage, and the driver wears a suit that's almost like a spacesuit in its protections. Bumping and rubbing is part of racing, but Ed thinks it goes too far these days. Too often, the shark breaks through. Racers once took pride in passing without touching, but now they'll pass any way they can.

"I tend to try to be old school, be a clean racer, but it's do or be done to," says Ed. A week after the Blewett brothers' wreck, Ted Christopher put Ed into the first turn wall at a different track, using the same tactics that killed John III. "You'd think we'd learn."

Ed was in the 2004 race at Thompson when Tommy Baldwin Sr. was killed sliding sideways into a concrete barrier surrounding a light pole in the infield. The grass was wet, and when Tommy's car slid off the track, it barely slowed down and hit the barrier full force on the driver's side.

When the race was stopped, the rest of the cars turned off their motors and sat on the track, waiting. They knew it was bad. After the ambulance left the track, and as the cleanup continued, Ed dropped the net, climbed out, and walked to Baldwin's crumpled car to try to understand how the accident had happened. He looked at the trajectory the car had taken and came to a conclusion: how would this *not* have happened.

Ed's all about safety on the track. After the Baldwin accident, the track redesigned the light poles and moved them up onto a berm out of harm's way, but Ed says NASCAR generally is too reactive and not proactive. After the Blewett wreck, Ed's team was the first to add another bar to the roll cage to protect the driver. NASCAR balked and wanted them to take it out, but the team refused. NASCAR has since come around.

Ed has stood before groups of drivers and talked about safety and driving issues, but for the most part, the message seems to be ignored or, worse, misinterpreted. At a meeting shortly after the Blewett brothers' wreck, Jimmy Blewett thought Ed was blaming him for his brother's death.

Ed sees a grief counselor. He's lost too many loved ones in the past year, most recently his mother. He had been taking out his anger and frustration on the track when friends urged him to seek help. It makes me wonder if the Hammond and Blewett families are seeing grief counselors. Maybe I should see one.

If you ask Ed why he drives a racecar, he says, "There's nothing better in the world to do." After the Blewett brothers' wreck, he was quoted in the *Courant*, saying that if anything happened to him, everyone should know that he died doing something he loved. Now he says, "I love racing, but I don't want to die in a racecar."

***

Ted Christopher walks with a spring in his step. Bespectacled, quick to smile, hair thinning on top but still dark brown with stray flecks of gray, at 50, he looks ten years younger, and he's not slowing down. Known simply as TC, he's raced everything and won everything from New Hampshire to Florida, from Sprint Cup to Three Quarter Midgets. "Prototypes at Daytona, Busch North, Busch South, trucks, Pro Stocks, Super Late Models, SKs, tour cars—a lot of different shit," says Ted. A grandstand at Stafford Motor Speedway is named after him, an honor usually reserved for legendary drivers who've passed on, such as Ed Flemke Sr., Richie Evans, and Bugsy Stevens. Ted qualified for AARP membership in June and married for the first time. "I guess it doesn't matter if I'm 50," he says. "It helps to have a 28-year-old wife."

Ted doesn't have a race shop as much as a complex. On the north side of the concrete parking lot is his business, the transmission shop that sells and services Allison transmissions, the heavy-duty gearbox that runs bulldozers, cement mixers, semis, dump trucks, and the behemoths of motorized transport. On the south side is the race shop, the mini-

Ted Christopher, left, listens to a crewmember.

cup shop he calls it.

Not superstitious, Ted would win his 100th race at Stafford Motor Speedway in his number 13 SK Modified on Friday the 13, making him the all-time winning driver in the history of the track. He's one of the most popular and controversial drivers in the region. People either love him or loathe him. As Pat discovered, he's a regular subject of graffiti on the women's bathroom walls at the track. Says Ted, "My wife told me that the first time she went racing. She says, 'Your name's on the wall in there.' I say, 'Oh, OK.'"

He sits at his computer in his office, which is crowded with trophies that overflow like a river of glitter from his desk onto the floor in front. Trophies of sterling silver, crystal, and brass sculpture, some as tall as a small child, others the size of a paperweight. There are die cast model cars of Dale's number 3 and a number 13 Late Model, racing helmets on top of the bookshelf, and a bottle of Advil within easy reach.

TC became notorious with his three-tap rule, his technique of getting a competitor's attention on the racetrack by bumping him, usually in a corner. "Number one: I'm here. Number two: you better pick a lane. Number three: I'll pick it for you. You know, I start in the back a lot of times. You move your way up to the top five or the top three, and there's a guy that's been there for the whole duration of the race. He's obviously not going anywhere, sometimes progressing backward, and then they jerk you around like crazy. Some of them even back up. Then they've got to fight you, so some of them you got to move out of the way. I consider if I move somebody and they catch me, they can move me if they want, but most of the time when I move somebody, I'm going forward, and they're staying where they are."

TC also achieved infamy by driving for Danbury trash hauler Jimmy Galante, who was investigated by the FBI, tried in federal court, and sent to prison for racketeering conspiracy, conspiracy to defraud the IRS, wire fraud conspiracy, and using New York Mafia muscle to protect his garbage collection territory. Among other holdings, Galante owned a minor-league hockey team and a shop full of racing equipment, including six racecars that Ted drove and housed.

"His stuff stayed here. It was all maintained in my shop, so I oversaw pretty much everything that went on."

When TC raced for Galante, he got to keep all his earnings as a driver and received an estimated budget of $600,000 to $800,000 a year, unprecedented for local short track racing. All that ended when the FBI showed up at his shop and hauled the cars and equipment away on flatbed trailers. "Yeah, search and seizure warrant. You and I are still paying for storage fees. Our crazy government; he's been in jail for seven months, the thing's over, and we're still paying $30,000 plus a year for those things to be stored. The tour stuff was a good deal with Jimmy when we had it. I became successful with Jimmy Galante. He was the best owner. There'll never be a better owner in this game. He was a good guy. He wants to come back." When he gets out, would Ted drive for him again? "Oh, yeah, we've already talked about that."

Ted and his twin brother, Mike, started racing karts when they were 18. Unlike most of the drivers, neither of the Christophers' parents nor any other relatives raced. The whole thing started as a mistake. The brothers had driven to Stafford Motor Speedway to watch the first race of the season but found that they had the date wrong. They were a week early. They knew there was a public kart track nearby, so on a whim they went racing and fell in love with it. From karts, they both went directly to racing SK Modifieds at Stafford and earned reputations as being hard driving and competitive. "It's not like nowadays where everybody buys a brand-new car, buys the best motor, buys a fire suit, somebody sets it up for them. All they got to do is learn how to drive the thing. Shit, first time I went to the track, all we did was do the toe. We didn't even scale the car. We didn't know anything, my brother and I, not one thing about racecars." Fans remember those days when more often than not, one brother would take the other out, or they'd both wind up in the fence. Mike retired from racing when he married and had a child. Ted, single, drove on.

Ted makes it a point to race every month of the year, and that's where the Three Quarter Midget comes in. "We only race it indoors. Indoor racing is fun, something to do in the wintertime, and it's been even more fun since we've been successful with it."

A full-size Midget—an oxymoron?—has a four-cylinder, 350-horsepower motor. A 750-liter motorcycle engine powers a TQ, and the car weighs less, but at first glance, it's hard to tell them apart.

Ted owns two cars now, his SK Modified and a backup. The backup is only an unpainted frame today, blending in against the raw metal surroundings. The SK is on a bright blue lift, the black, white, and red color scheme standing out in the shop. He has a different crew for every division. The only factor that stays the same is Ted.

His philosophy of driving a racecar is simple: "Try to win every race, make my car better as the weeks go. You know, keep the wheels on it." He admits he doesn't like following cars but that it's satisfying to start in the back. "I'm very good at passing people. I've done that throughout my whole career. That's probably one of my better attributes."

The worst wreck he's been in? "I've been knocked out a few times. I've wrecked some cars really bad. Probably one of the worst wrecks was at Waterford. Yeah, a guy spun out and then came back onto the track, and when he came back out onto the track, he catapulted me. Straight up in the air. I was as high as the flagman. The thing went straight up in the air and was sitting there like this, and it was the same height as the fence. I got pictures of it. Crazy. Then it came down, crashed, and wrecked. Yeah, that was a pretty ugly one."

Ted has made money in racing, especially when he was racing for Galante. "My accountant always said, 'Don't stop racing for that guy.'"

Ted Christopher is comfortable with himself and where he is at the 50-year mark. New wife, new resolve, and a new season bring a big smile when he says, "I don't care if you hate me or you like me as long as you appreciate my talent behind the wheel."

Talented drivers can emerge at a very young age; some spend their weekends on the racetrack and their weekdays in kindergarten. When I was young, I drew pictures of racecars. Today, kids young enough to need a baby-sitter are driving racecars in competition and driving them hard.

It Starts Early

A passing thunderstorm threatens, but the weather hasn't dissuaded maybe 50 Quarter Midget teams from showing up at the Silver City Quarter Midget Club. Some of the trailers in the parking lot have two or three pint-sized racecars in them. The sparkling clean repair shop inside one trailer rivals anything on the grown-up, major-league touring circuit. Campers are parked everywhere, and the license plates are from all over the East Coast. This is the Little League of racing, although these parents make Little League baseball parents look comatose. This is a hands-on, intense, emotional sport for the entire family.

Silver City's verdant, park-like racetrack advertises that it's in Meriden, Connecticut. It's actually in South Meriden. The leafy borough bills itself as "Home of the South Meriden Volunteer Fire Dept." How competitive are these drivers? Imagine Jeff Gordon—who started out racing Quarter Midgets—condense him to half size, even make him a girl. That describes most of the drivers here this morning. Some are as young as 5 and range in age up to 16, but the younger kids' divisions dominate today. Many of the older kids have 11 years of racing experience behind them by the time they hit their junior year in high school.

The young drivers walk around confidently in their professional-looking little driver's suits and HANS devices, their helmets larger than the wheels on their cars. They take off their driving gloves and throw them nonchalantly into the cockpits. There's a confidence about them already, a spring in their step just like Ted Christopher's. They know that Sprint Cup drivers Bobby Labonte and Ryan Newman also started their careers in Quarter Midgets. The girls talk about Danica Patrick, who raced karts as a kid, but both boys and girls look to Joey Logano—who started racing here at Silver City as a 6-year-old—as their role model. Others dare not dream that high. Going local would be fun enough for them.

The drivers already know that all these grown-ups, from the flagman to the pit crew, are there to serve them. A car has mechanical trouble and drives into the pits. With the driver still in it, two large dads tip it sideways to fix the problem underneath. A car stalls after a spin on the track; a dad—a corner man—runs out to push start it. In the pits, a small driver sits in his car, which sits on a rack on top of a small pit box. Two dads lift the car and driver off the rack and carry it several feet, like servants carrying a potentate in a sedan chair.

It's a learning environment: how to line up for starts and restarts, how to pass, what to do in the turns, how to find the line, when to stop, when to keep going, what the flags mean, how to wait for your turn to drive onto the track, how to compete in a race, what dad's trackside hand signals mean. The kids are learning to handle not only their cars but also their parents. Some parents are more excitable than others. Many have high expectations for their child drivers. They say they just want to have fun, but some people don't have fun unless they win. That can put a lot of pressure on a kid.

The pressure's on dad too. At the very least, he needs to have some kind of mechanical ability, or the kid will be at a huge disadvantage. It helps if dad has a sharp racing instinct too. Certainly, mom is important to the team, which couldn't function without her support, but, as in all racing, men dominate. It's primal for dad—how he fathers, how much he can provide for his kid with his own talent, knowledge, and money. He doesn't want to let the kid down by not providing a competitive car, and the kid doesn't want to let dad down by not winning. For a kid, there's nothing like being the center of dad's attention or just spending time with him. Fathers are mysterious, frightening sometimes, the biggest, baddest animals on the planet. When they bellow, it goes right to the trembling heart of a kid.

My father scared the hell out of me. Still does. He has a quick temper when he goes up against frustration. It comes in a flash in the middle of a sentence, or it builds step-by-step and explodes into a red-faced growl. Even now, when he angrily rails about a neighbor who neglects a pet dog, I get that shot of alarm adrenaline.

In the Silver City pits, three ponytailed, pre-teen girls in driver's suits gather in a small circle next to a car. They're talking about driving techniques; they're bending and stretching, giggling, a present-day Degas scene without the tutus and ballet slippers. No floor to ceiling mirrors or ballet barres but plenty of roll bars. Instead of leotards and leg warmers, T-shirts under fire suits, the tops draped casually from the waist, tightly wrapped buns loosened into ponytails. How aware are the girls of the boys?

Modified driver Renee Dupuis raced at Silver City when she was a kid, setting six track records and winning five driver-of-the-year awards. "I'm not sure at exactly what age I started to realize it was more than just driver versus driver, but it was well before my tenth birthday. It certainly was boy versus girl back in Quarter Midgets. They even had separate boy and girl driver-of-the-year awards. The boy versus girl situation very much continues today."

After each heat, the cars are weighed with the drivers. The weigh station is a small wooden shed open at both ends so the cars can be quickly and easily pushed in over the scales and out the other doorway. There's a sign at the entrance: "These premises are monitored by video. No cash allowed inside."

The oval track is 1/20 of a mile around, and the cars can hit 30 to 50 miles an hour, depending on the division. As in all open-wheel racing, the cars wreck when the wheels touch. Some wrecks are spectacular and singularly frightening—a little kid is inside that roll cage.

In one heat, two cars get into each other on the backstretch, one vaulting into the air. It lands upright—no harm done. The race continues, but on the next lap, two cars tangle and one rolls over, stopping upside down. The crowd hushes as the corner men and officials leap over the chain-link fence and race to the accident. They turn the car upright and crowd around it, so many large men that they block the view for a moment. "Are you OK?" they ask loudly over the buzz of motors. There is silence in the stands; the spectators hold a collective breath, straining to hear the answer. Yes, she's OK. She finishes the race, coming in second. Later, a spectator asks her, "What's it like to flip?" She couldn't have been older than 11; her ponytail bounces she walks in front of the grandstand. Smiling, blushing at the question from a stranger, she says, "It's fun."

The racecars are organized into 14 classes and divisions ranging from the youngest newbie to the oldest experienced drivers. Safety is paramount, and the national Quarter Midget Association says the sport is safer than Little League football. The whole family is involved. If a family member is not directly involved in keeping the car running, she's in the stands cheering, reading her Harry Potter book between races.

The cars cost $3,000 to $4,500 new, less if used. A typical motor is the perennial workhorse Briggs & Stratton, but Honda and Continental/Deco make reliable motors too. The motors may not be souped up and may be repaired only with approved parts. The cars are direct drive, like the full-size Midgets and Supermodifieds at the big tracks. They're chain driven and have no transmissions, and the rear power wheels are hard to turn because they're connected to the motor. To push the car is to turn everything in the drive train. After one heat race, I see a young driver trying to push his car to the weigh station, but he's too small and the car is too stubborn. It barely moves. Maybe his pit dad is helping a sibling or is a corner man and can't leave his post. Another young driver—a competitor in the race that just ended—comes over and helps the kid, the two pushing it easily. Everyone helps each other at Silver City. After all, they're in a club.

Racing With Jesus

Father God, in the name of our Lord and Savior, Jesus, we ask for your hand of protection on us. We ask that Your Spirit will guide our actions and that we would respond in a way that will honor you. Give us your wisdom, patience, and guidance. We thank you for answering our prayers. In Jesus' name, amen. — Driver's Prayer

Reverend Don Rivers and Reverend Dan Petfield have been to dozens of races together as preachers in Racing With Jesus Ministries, a traveling speedway church that visits racetracks with NASCAR touring divisions throughout the East and the South in a gold-and-purple Dodge pace car and satin-sheen jackets to match. Reverend Pat Evans started Racing With Jesus Ministries in 1980 with encouragement from the king, Richard Petty. He thought the NASCAR tour drivers and crews could use a conscience and needed a little salvation. In RWJM, they say, "Our congregation travels at 150 miles an hour and turns left." Like evangelicals everywhere, they sell Jesus to the masses, but even the doubters respect them.

On April 6, Reverend Don, stocky, dark hair, with the affable good looks of a mainstream minister, was watching the winged Midgets scream into turn three at Thompson.

Reverend Dan, younger and shorter, had his eyes on Erica Santos diving low into turn four. The reverends were at the track to minister to the Whelen Tour and were strictly spectators for the other divisions.

Rev. Don Rivers

Reverend Don says that when he saw the accident, his mind went blank. He wasn't sure what he had seen just a split second earlier: cars spinning between turn three and four, everything happening at once, a car flying into the air, cartwheeling over the wall. He was sure the car had cleared the wall and rolled down the embankment on the other side. He could see it happen in his mind's eye: the small car flipping end over end, shedding parts until it stops in the open field, on its side, the driver crawling out, raising both hands to show he's all right. That kind of winged Midget wreck happens often enough and is spectacular. Reverend Don elbowed his companion and pointed to turn three. The car had cleared the wall but hadn't cleared the Budweiser sign. It was jammed grotesquely into the heavy black steel stanchion on the right side.

Reverend Dan saw the white smoke rising from the invisible flaming methanol leaking from the car. When he saw the reaction of the safety crew, he got a horrible sinking feeling inside. The car was stuck 4 feet above the wall, smoke rising lazily, almost serenely, from the wreck. Both reverends had seen these kinds of wrecks before, and they knew it was bad. Reverend Dan wanted to go back to the NEMA pits on the far side of the track behind the back straightaway but hesitated because he didn't know anyone in the organization. The two ministers traveled with the NASCAR Camping World East and Whelen Modified Tours. They knew those people. They were friends.

"Reverend Don encouraged me to go back there and see what I could do to help," Reverend Dan says.

"I knew it wasn't good," says Reverend Don. "You know these things when you see them." He had seen Adam Petty, Tommy Baldwin, Kenny Irwin, and John Blewett die on racetracks. He thought back to the 2007 season. "John Blewett's accident wasn't that way. I fully expected John to walk away." Reverend Don has seen enough fatal racing accidents that he knew exactly what to do. I told him I'd never seen anything like that before, how shocked I had been, and asked him how he could function.

"You enter a zone of sorts that allows you to separate yourself from the incident and focus on who needs to be reached out to. I think it's God enabling us to do his work and provide comfort for those who need it." Both say they dealt with their own grief later, alone in prayer.

Reverend Dan headed for the NEMA pits while Reverend Don intercepted a friend of Shane's, one of the very few people he knew in the winged Midget world. Reverend Don knew this man would need help. He was right. The man––a past NEMA champion, car owner, test driver, and instructor, sat in his truck, crying, driving toward the pit gate, trying to escape his feelings and confusion, not wanting to know what he knew. Reverend Don flagged the man down, climbed into the truck, talked to him for a while, and prayed with him. Afterward, the man said he had to go home. He said he needed time alone.

Meanwhile, Reverend Dan walked through the NEMA pits in his purple, black, and gold jacket, "Racing With Jesus" emblazoned across the front and back, a stylized cross part of the design. The rest of the winged Midget race was canceled.

Cars were coming off the track now, pushed by pickup trucks and ATVs. Stunning disbelief hung in the cold air. Officials, crewmembers, and drivers approached the minister, wanting to talk. "I was there for them. I did my best to encourage and strengthen those who needed it." He consoled Shane's grandfather, Jack Glockner, Shane's role model. Many of the winged Midget drivers who were in the race unbuckled their harnesses and climbed out of their cars to gather around the minister—one of them was Shane's best friend, Randy Cabral. Reverend Dan led them in prayer while tears ran down the faces of the young drivers, their helmets still on, their visors still down, their hearts broken.

Announcements came over the pit speakers. "Whelen Tour, line up." Line up for the next race, the Whelen Tour 150-lap feature race for the Modifieds. Keep going as if nothing had happened. Put it out of your mind. Maintain the schedule. Drivers came from hundreds of miles away to race this day. They paid their fees. The stands are full of paying customers. Let's go. The ministers comforted Shane's friends Ryan Preece and Bobby Santos III, who were about to go on the track in a tour Modified.

"Drivers can compartmentalize," says Reverend Don. "But sometimes the lines cross." Just before he was to give the invocation for the start of the Whelen Tour race, Reverend Dan got word that Shane had died on the way to the hospital. The minister wasn't allowed to make an announcement, because family members have to be notified first. Shane's stepfather was not at the track; neither was his father. What could the minister say?

"I asked the Lord to give me wisdom for that prayer," Reverend Dan says. He prayed that God would give strength and wisdom to the people involved in the wreck.

The show must go on. The winged Midget tour must continue, another day, a new track. These things happen in racing; everyone knows that drivers sometimes die. Load up the cars, put them on the trailers, pack away the tools and extra tires. There are schedules to keep, put together in the off-season; there are agreements and contracts. The following week, there's another first race of the season at another track, the Waterford Speedbowl. Randy Cabral will win the NEMA feature at the Bowl and tearfully dedicate the victory to Shane.

Jesus Scares Me, This I Know

My parents divorced when I was 10. Divorce is common now, but back then, Tim and I were the only kids in the neighborhood without a father living in the house. Feeling the loss, I began spending more time with a family in the neighborhood. Everyone's first name began with *D*. The D's lived in an older, barn-like, two-story house at the top of the hill on Bowser Avenue, a quiet, tree-lined street named after the Fort Wayne inventor of the first gasoline pump. Their yard was a double lot, the biggest in the neighborhood. The sandbox, shaded by a maple tree, was the size of my bedroom. The retired couple next door grew rhubarb next to a peach tree near the alley.

The children were two boys and a girl. I hung out with the boys—Darwin, who was my age, and Dwight, a little younger. I'd known them my whole life. We had been tearing up the sidewalks racing down that steep hill in Darwin's red wagon since we were 7 years old, back during the Korean War. One day when we were playing in Darwin and Dwight's front yard, another neighborhood kid, an older girl, asked,

"Did you know there's a war going on?" We looked up to see if we could spot some bombers flying in formation like the ones we saw in World War II movies. We saw only blue sky and puffy clouds.

Darwin and Dwight's family belonged to the First Assembly of God Church and went to every Sunday morning service and Wednesday night prayer meeting. They were evangelical, born-again Christians who believed that Jesus was coming back any second and God have mercy on your soul if he caught you sinning. The sin list was long—no smoking, drinking, swearing, making oaths, or going to movies of any kind. Comic books were banned. All were sins. God have further mercy on your soul if you were a woman and Jesus came back and caught you wearing makeup.

I didn't care about their religion one way or another, and I had no idea what *born again* meant. I had seen my little brother when he came home all pink and crying from the hospital after he was born. How could he be born again? I liked Darwin and Dwight, their toys, the big sandbox, their parents, the occasional dinners, the sour rhubarb and sweet ripe peaches next door. They were only a block away up the hill, but going to their house was like going on vacation. They made me one of the family, and I was feeling the loss of mine.

"How would you like to go to church with us on Sunday?" asked Dale, the dad. I told him I would, that I didn't think my mother would mind, that it might give her a moment's peace to know her oldest was interested in church. She was miserable most of the time, and I thought maybe my going to church would cheer her up. On Sunday morning, they picked me up, and we rode to the church laughing, four kids squeezed into the back seat, parents up front, like a family.

The church was a large, rectangular, concrete-block

and brick building. It had two stories and was architecturally unimaginative inside and out. There was a cross at the front of the sanctuary but no statues, paintings, or artwork of any kind, no distractions, save for the congregation. I'd never seen a spectacle like it. I had gone to my grandparents' church a few times with my family, a typically subdued Protestant congregation with a matching minister. It was all very mannerly, quiet even.

The preacher at my friends' church yelled his sermons. He started softly, friendly enough, but it didn't take long before he was howling in ecstasy, red-faced, his forehead drenched in holy sweat. By then, the congregation had begun to stir. Every now and then, someone would raise both hands to the ceiling and shout "Amen" or "Praise Jesus," and soon the shouts became a roar of crying, wailing, moaning people. They sang loudly, as beautifully as they could; nobody held back.

The minister warned the crowd about sinning but shouted that Jesus would forgive them if they'd let him into their hearts. "Who wants to accept Jesus Christ as their lord and savior this morning?" he cried out. A dozen people filed slowly, humbly to the altar. "Who needs healing?" he thundered. More people went up. "Who wants their sins washed away by the blood of the lamb?" Soon, a steady stream of sinners filled the aisles, shuffling to the front.

The minister put his hand on top of the head of each sick person. "Heal in the name of Jesus Christ," he bellowed as he slammed his open palm onto the sick person's forehead. Many of the healed collapsed at the preacher's feet. I watched people overcome with passion faint in the aisles, some swaying in their pews, falling exhausted into their seats. I was fascinated, not by the religion but by the people, the families, the commotion. I became a regular.

The same people went up week after week. Every Sunday,

I saw people speaking in tongues, hands raised, praising Jesus, crying, falling, moaning. They seemed to be terrified of dying, yet they wanted Jesus to come back now, today, and lift them up, to take them home so they could live forever.

I had conquered death when I was 6. I'd prayed to my own Jesus without guidance from the First Assembly of God Church, and he had heard me, healed me, and made me healthy again. Well, the doctor and the soldiers in the fort had helped, but now I was 11 years old with my life ahead of me. I had plenty of fears, but dying wasn't one of them.

Going to this church almost every Sunday slowly, imperceptibly changed that. I began to be more afraid. It was bad enough having divorced parents, but a new fear entered my life. Of what, I didn't know. Of being caught? Being caught at what? I wasn't sure, but I must've done something wrong. I didn't dance or smoke, so it couldn't have been that. I'd say an occasional swearword for laughs with friends on my block, but it wasn't a habit. Maybe it was my comic books, maybe the cowboy movies I watched on TV. The constant message from the pulpit was that we were all sinners and that we sinned even when we didn't know we were sinning. I could understand pointing the finger at adults—they had a lot to atone for—but kids? Me? What had I done to warrant this sin? My mother cried all the time, and she had appointed me man of the house. I was supposed to be able to fix things, yet I couldn't. Was that a sin? I couldn't stop reading comic books. I spent the night at my cousin's house once and read all his *Tales from the Crypt* comic books. My father had been taking Tim and me to the movies nearly once a week since the divorce. That must be it—going to movies. I was a sinner. The preacher had told me so.

Yes, it was all there. I was a sinner. My mother was a sinner because she wore makeup, my father was a sinner because he swore, my 5-year-old brother was a sinner because he had been born, and I was a sinner because I went to movies.

The First Assembly of God had a club called Sky Pilots that was like Cub Scouts for boys fascinated with airplanes. We met once a week to build model airplanes out of balsa wood and tissue paper. We memorized Bible verses––"devotions," the leader called them. Jesus was our co-pilot, and every week the leader reminded us that the Lord was coming back any second, that the end of the world was near, and that if Jesus caught me dancing, swearing, kissing a girl, or watching a movie, he'd punish me, and I'd go straight to hell. I went to a Wednesday afternoon Bible class in the neighborhood too, which sent the same message. Eventually, the climate of fear took its toll.

Every time I saw a particularly dramatic cloud formation in the sky, I expected Jesus to appear on a golden ray of sunlight descending to Earth. I didn't want that to happen. I liked my life; I didn't want to leave Earth. I had worked hard to stay here, followed the doctor's orders, taken my medicine, stayed in bed, and protected the fort from the Indians. I had toys, a two-wheeled bike, a baseball and a new glove, and a fairly complete baseball card collection. The White Sox were having a good year. I continued to try very hard to reconcile the First Assembly of God's Jesus with my personal experience.

When I was 8 years old, somebody stole my bike from the front yard while my grandfather was baby-sitting. He put Tim and me in the car, and we drove around the neighborhood to see if we could find it. While he drove, I prayed quietly to myself, "Please, Jesus, let me find my bike"—and there it was, lying on its side in a yard four blocks down the street. The paperboy had taken it. Grandpa pulled the car over, jumped out, and cornered the kid, grabbing him by the collar. "You want me to call the cops?" he asked. I looked at the frightened kid on the verge of tears, maybe five years older than me.

"No, I just want my bike back."

From that day on, I was a firm believer in Jesus Christ. This new version of him at the First Assembly of God, this punisher, this judging, threatening, vengeful God was a stranger to me, but if I wanted to be part of a family, even though my name didn't start with a *D*, I had to get with the program.

The oldest son of the preacher at the First Assembly of God had the same problem every preacher's kid has—the pressure to be good. He was in Sky Pilots and my Sunday school class. He was a year older than me, friendly and polite to everyone, quiet, confident, mannerly. I didn't know what he was like away from the church until I went to church camp for a week that summer. This was the first time I'd been away from home without being with blood relatives. We swam and canoed, played volleyball and tennis—the usual summer camp activities with the addition of reading Bible stories and singing hymns. At night in our cabin, when the adult supervisor was in a different bunkhouse with the other counselors, the PK would start in with the vilest language. He talked about boy and girl body parts, using words I'd never heard before. I had learned a few choice phrases from my older cousins in rural Huntertown, but I can trace most of my knowledge of vulgar names of body parts back to the PK at church camp. When I came home, my mother asked,

"What'd you learn at camp?"

"How to swim," I said.

Tim and I looked forward to our father's weekly visits. On Thursday evenings, we went to Grandma and Grandpa's house for dinner. On a Saturday, we'd go to the movies downtown in the daytime and maybe a drive-in movie at night. At first, I didn't tell my father about the beliefs at the First Assembly of God because I wanted to be with him as much as possible, and I wasn't sure he'd approve. If it meant risking eternal damnation, I'd take the chance. One Saturday afternoon, we went to see *Old Yeller* at the Embassy downtown, the nicest movie theater in the city, a palace. The spotlight lit the stage, the music started, and the giant Page theater organ, white with gilded trim, rose out of the orchestra pit for a short pre-movie concert. About a third of the way through the movie—long before the young boy has to shoot his rabid dog—I started crying. After these many months, I couldn't hold it in anymore. I was terrified.

"What's wrong?" asked Dad.

"I'm afraid," I said.

"Of what?"

"Jesus."

"Jesus? What are you talking about?"

"Jesus is going to come back and catch me here in the movies, and I'm going to go to hell."

"Come back? What do you mean come back? Come back from where?"

"From heaven. He's coming back any minute. These are the end times, the end of the world. He's coming back, and we're all going to hell."

"Who told you that?"

"Sky Pilots, the church, the preacher, everybody." People around us began to shush us, whispering to us to be quiet.

"We'll talk about it later," said Dad.

"No, I want to go now."

"No. Watch the goddam movie."

By the time the boy put the dog out of his misery, I was frantic. We filed out of the auditorium along with crying children and their parents, but I was crying for an entirely different reason. When we were outside, I looked for a cloud formation in the sky that might give me a warning.

"Now, what's all that bullshit about movies?" asked Dad as he lit a cigarette—another sin by the way. My father had always been good at putting certain religions into perspective for me with one word, usually *bullshit*. One time some of my friends in the neighborhood—all Catholics—told me that I wasn't going to heaven because I wasn't a Roman Catholic. It started a big argument, and I ran home and told this new information to my father.

"Bullshit," he said. "They've got babies sleeping in dresser drawers down there. They don't know a goddam thing."

After the movie, we had ice cream and went home. My father dropped us off in the driveway. He didn't get out of the car or come to the door; he didn't talk with my mother anymore. Whenever they tried to have a conversation, whether on the phone or in person, they got into a screaming match.

Two weeks later, my mother took me to see the minister at the brand-new Methodist Church built two blocks from my house. The large A-frame structure still smelled of fresh paint and varnish. The minister met us at his office door. He was older, in his early 50s maybe. His dark hair was flecked with gray, and he had blue eyes and a sweet face. He was friendly and kind, his hands as soft and pink as the pope's. I thought that God—Jesus's dad—would look like this minister. My mother sat on a chair outside in the hall while I went alone into the minister's office. He closed the door, and there were just the two of us.

Books lined the shelves; a houseplant filled a corner. I sat in the big comfortable leather chair that faced the minister. We talked about the White Sox, baseball cards, football, school, and comic books; then we got around to movies. He said, "I'm a minister. I know Jesus very well, and you know what? He doesn't care if you go to the movies." He didn't have to parse his words. There was only one kind of movie in Fort Wayne in 1956—no sex, no profanity, and no gore.

"I know Jesus," he continued, "and I know he wants you to continue to be a good boy and enjoy your life. That's all he wants. Enjoy your movies, your comic books, your White Sox. You can even dance if you want to." I had no interest in dancing. "There's nothing wrong with any of it," he said. "You have God's blessing. You have Jesus's blessing." When I went to bed that night, I felt relieved for the first time in months.

After that day, I stopped going to First Assembly of God and the Wednesday Bible class. I didn't hang around as much with Darwin and Dwight and slowly drifted away from them and their family as I got older. I began to think of my mother as my family, my only family. I had wanted my father to help me somehow, to save me from the evangelists, to say the magic one-liner that would cut me loose. He did nothing. He didn't even live in my house anymore. My mother took me to the minister.

I didn't find out until many years later that my father had gone to a midweek service at the First Assembly of God to check it out for himself. Appalled after one visit, he arranged my meeting with the Methodist minister to deprogram me. He made it happen. I was a graybeard in my 50s when he revealed the truth to me. That's the advantage of a long life.

My father is not a boastful man, not willing to discuss his good deeds or his triumphs. In his prime, he was a great amateur golfer, shot in the middle 70s as a young man and low 80s when he got older. In all the times I've played with him, I've never heard him brag about a well-played shot, and I've seen plenty.

I didn't know until I became an adult that World War II was the source of his rage, the things he saw, his friends who died. He wants to talk about it today but can't. Tears fill his eyes, and his voice drifts off to change the subject.

Once I said to him, "You World War II guys don't talk about anything. The Vietnam vets, all they want to do is talk about their experiences, but you World War II guys don't say squat." He said, "Well, we weren't supposed to!"

I took that to mean he was under orders to not say anything—everything the OSS did was secret—but I also took it to mean men of his generation didn't talk about their demons, whether they had been in the war or not. They were supposed to suck it up and walk on the sunny side of the street. Buck up, bucko. Don't be a crybaby; don't show you're weak. Be like Gary Cooper, the strong, silent type.

I knew nothing of that when I was a confused, frightened 11-year-old. All I knew was that my parents were divorced, my mother was in a foul mood all the time, and Tim and I were fatherless, the only kids in the neighborhood in that unlucky boat. I had my art, though, and I immersed myself in it.

And the Winner Is

Iwas having that last magical summer of pre-adolescence, between sixth grade and seventh, before tyrannical hormones would run my life. I was at the end of male child existence, of boyness. I was 12 and flipping back and forth between playing with toy cars in my sandbox in the daytime and dreaming about naked girls at night. I made oil paintings in an art class with older teenagers on Saturday mornings and played Air Force, Army, or racecar driver with Terry—my friend since kindergarten—in the afternoons.

I often baby-sat Tim while my mother worked, and sometimes Terry helped. We made hamburgers for lunch by throwing raw patties against the kitchen ceiling to flatten them before cooking.

None of the men my mother dated could stand up to Tim's and my high standards except one. It helped that he bribed the judges. What put Chester Shropshire over the top was that he always brought us a six-pack of Pepsi and a bag of potato chips when he came to visit. That was all we needed.

I don't know how long they dated—it didn't seem very

long—but one day, Mom sat Tim and me down and said she was going to marry Chet. Tim, 7 years old then, was happy she had chosen the right guy, but I burst out crying. I was 12 years old, smoking cigarettes with friends in the outside stairwells at my school behind our house, dreaming of naked girls at night, daydreaming about driving a car someday, and I cried like a little baby.

"What's wrong?" asked Mom. "I thought you liked him."

"I do like him," I said, "but I won't be the man of the house anymore."

My mother married Chet in a small ceremony somewhere out of town, Churubusco I think it was. Tim and I weren't invited. Instead, our father took us to Grandma and Grandpa's house for the day. Stepfather. It was weird, disturbing even, as if I had been adopted suddenly. What was even more disturbing was being a stepson. To me, that sounded like a kid with only one leg.

Chet was divorced. He had two daughters younger than me, a sister, a brother in California, and three brothers nearby who were married with children. With the step-aunts, step-uncles, and step-cousins, the size of my family seemed to double overnight. Chet's brothers and their families came over often, or we visited them. The grown-ups played a card game called euchre, which as near as I could tell involved slamming cards on the table and drinking a lot of beer.

One of Chet's brothers, Charlie, and his wife, Marge, had no children but owned a farm, life imitating art again. Back in the fourth grade, I had invented an aunt and uncle who owned a farm and an airplane. On Mondays, the teacher asked us what we had done over the weekend. When it was my turn, I told the class I had gone flying with my uncle. I described my adventure in great detail. I even drew pictures of it, the big red barn, the haystacks, the warm, cozy white farmhouse with a big front porch and plenty of horses, pigs, cows, and chickens. The plane was a yellow Piper Cub J-3-F-50 with a black lightning bolt running down the side. I had seen a picture of it in a magazine. My real uncles then worked for the railroad or in factories. None of them lived on a farm or had an airplane, but my fantasy was more fun than boring reality.

One night, my mother went to a parent-teacher conference at school. When she came home, she asked, "What's this about an uncle and a farm and an airplane?" She tried to be stern, but she wound up having a good laugh about it. I asked her if I should apologize to my teacher, and she said to just not talk about it anymore. Now, years later, I had an aunt and uncle who owned a farm. Well, step-aunt and step-uncle and no airplane but a farm that looked very much the way I had drawn it.

We started going to South Anthony Speedway every Saturday night with my new stepfamily. This brought more authenticity to my drawings of racecars, things I hadn't known before, such as how loud the cars at the track were, which didn't translate over the radio, TV, or speakers in the movies. I'd had no idea they made so much noise. The cars weren't muffled, and on a clear night, I could hear them 3 miles away. I'd heard them in the past, way off in the distance, but hadn't known what that sound was. I'd thought it was just part of the summer night sounds, mostly chirping crickets, train whistles, and the chugging of steam engines. Now I knew.

When the cars wrecked, the impact sounded nothing like the wrecks in the movies, with that squealing tire sound and the rolling crunch of metal and smashing glass, maybe a hubcap spinning to a stop. Oddly, in reality, it wasn't dramatic, just a metallic thud, like the sound of slamming the hood shut on the family car. For a kid who was afraid of loud noises, I was ironically attracted to these cars, except for the backfires. If I knew a certain car was going to backfire as the driver lifted going into a turn, I put my fingers in my ears.

My mother, stepfather, step-aunts, and step-uncles sat in the stands, drinking beer and chain-smoking cigarettes, while we kids played hide-and-seek and tag between races. My new stepsisters and step-cousins—except for the boy step-cousin who was about my age—were younger than me, but I felt OK about slipping into kid's games, even at the advanced age of 12. However, when the cars lined up on the track for a heat race or a feature, we stopped whatever we were doing and watched the action.

South Anthony Speedway was a 3/8-mile asphalt bull-ring that held races on Tuesdays and Saturdays. Drivers named Cowboy Likes, Cozy Coe, Barney Barnhill, Buck Beezley, Duke Krocker, and Hook Henderson drove Modifieds. There were no other divisions. I liked a driver named Dick Salesman, but one driver always made us laugh when the announcer said his name: Skeeter Grocock. The younger kids didn't know what we were laughing about. "What's so funny?" one of my girl step-cousins or a stepsister would ask.

"Grow cock," my male step-cousin and I would say with adolescent cackles. "Grow. Cock." We were 12.

The Modifieds were chopped up, stripped-down junk-yard refugees from the 1930s and '40s, usually old Plymouths, Fords, Chevys, or Crosley coupes but powered by souped-up, big block V-8 motors from Chevy, Ford, Cadillac, Lincoln, and Hudson. There were no motor rules; some motors had three two-barrel carburetors, some had two, and some were fuel injected. There were few restrictions on the chassis and body. Instead of gasoline, the cars ran on a mixture of alcohol, nitro-methane, and castor oil, the same fuel used in model airplane motors today. They turned slightly slower times than today's Mods, but even at those speeds, there were plenty of wrecks, spins, and cars flying over the wall. I don't remember an ambulance ever taking anyone away.

The drivers were valiant gods dressed in T-shirts. Safety equipment was a thin white helmet, blue jeans, motorcycle boots, Air Force–type goggles, and a military surplus lap belt. There were no roll cages, special driver's seats, five-point harnesses, HANS devices, nerf bars, or fire extinguishers. Salesman was famous for driving one-handed—right hand on the steering wheel, left elbow on the window sash, and a cigar stub in his mouth. As much as I fantasized about being a racecar driver, I had never met one. The only driver I knew was Eddie Doyle.

Eddie Doyle was handsome, with the strong jaw and small nose of a comics-page hero. He had dark hair and plenty of it. He was clean-shaven but sometimes skipped a shave before a big race, such as Le Mans or Indy. He had several girlfriends, whom he kissed hard, intensely. I knew nothing of those pleasures at the time, but Eddie Doyle got me my first kiss.

Mr. Brumbaugh, my sixth-grade teacher, decided our class would publish a weekly newspaper. It would be mimeographed in purple ink on letter-sized paper and feature news, views, and, of course, a comic strip—*Eddie Doyle*.

It was an adventure strip. I was a fan of three adventure strips: *Joe Palooka*, by Ham Fisher; *Steve Canyon*, by Milt Caniff; and *Steve Roper*, by Bill Overgard and Allen Saunders. They were written to appeal to boys, were drawn to perfection, and had exciting story lines, plenty of action, and beautiful, sexy women with large breasts. Joe Palooka was a boxer, and Steve Canyon was an Air Force pilot. Steve Roper was a newspaper reporter, and his tough-guy sidekick was a character named Mike Nomad. Eddie Doyle looked like Steve Roper in a racing helmet.

The comic strip was a hit from day one. My friends asked

me during the week what would happen in the next install-
ment of the story, and I'd tell them they had to wait until the
next issue of the paper to find out. Truth was, I didn't know
myself. Eddie Doyle lived in my imagination every day, but
it was odd to bring him into the real world. He was more
intensely mine, part of the universe inside my head, when I
was drawing pictures in the privacy of my bedroom. Now I
had opened the characters that lived inside my brain to all
my sixth-grade classmates. It turned out to be very cool.

We were the baby boom generation, the post–World
War II mob of children invading the unprepared school systems of America. There were more of us than Merle J. Ab-
bett Elementary School could hold. The board of education
tried staggering the dates for children entering kindergarten—some went in September and some in January—and
dividing the grades into A and B. I was in grade 6B. Classes
overflowed, and the school district built temporary classrooms at almost every school in the system.

My classroom was inside a metal, barn-like structure behind the school. It had a tall ceiling and wooden floors and
was very noisy, voices echoing, books opening and closing,
and a general hum bouncing off the metal walls. The building was divided into two sixth-grade classrooms separated
by an entry hall. We had the usual fire drills and tornado
drills, but the one that puzzled us the most was the nuclear
attack drill. The Cold War between the United States and
the Soviet Union was in full bloom. We saw black-and-
white movies in class about nuclear explosions that leveled
pretty much everything in a 50-mile radius. The firestorm
alone destroyed every carbon-based object in sight, but
somehow, crawling under our desks and putting our heads
between our knees would protect us from an atom bomb.
Eddie Doyle's adventures were the only thing that made
sense to a lot of us kids.

A classmate I had my eye on—she had dark eyes, dark hair, and a mature figure—was a fan of the strip. One day at recess, she told me so. Her name was Susan, and I suggested that possibly I might come over some Friday night to visit at her house a few blocks away. She agreed, and on Friday night, I was there in her living room.

The room was hot, or maybe it was just me. Susan had a younger sibling still in diapers and an older sister named Claudia, who was in an intense argument with their mother. I didn't know whether the toddler was a boy or a girl, but I got there right after a change. The smell was ripe, the room was hot, and I thought I was going to be sick. Susan suggested we sit in the enclosed porch on the back of the house where we could be alone.

It felt cooler there. We sat next to each other on an old couch. I put my arm around her and asked her if she'd ever kissed a boy. She said she hadn't. My heart pounded. I had gone to the edge. Jump.

"Hold on to your hat," I said, and I kissed her. It was warm, wet, and electric. That's all, just one kiss. I thought that was plenty. I had crossed a threshold and couldn't go back, yet I was not quite ready to forge on. I was stuck in that pre-adolescent, near post-boyhood purgatory.

Susan and I didn't exactly go steady, but there was a bond between us. I put her in the strip as Eddie Doyle's girlfriend. I visited her home several times and got more kisses, but the sandbox in my backyard still called to me.

The comic strip ended in June when we left the sixth grade for summer vacation. Eddie Doyle occupied my imagination in equal measure alongside increasing fantasies about girls, but at that time, boyhood won out, and soon I was back playing in the sandbox with Terry.

We let our imaginations run wild. We were Air Force pilots, racecar drivers, and soldiers. When we weren't play-

ing at my house, we were at Terry's. We put firecrackers inside our model planes and military vehicles and blew them
up. We listened to foreign radio stations on the big powerful shortwave radio in his basement. Terry sneaked out of
bed one night and saw his parents watching a pornographic
movie in the living room. He told me all about it. None of
it made sense to either one of us, but the world was opening
up. Adult secrets were being exposed little by little.

Near the end of summer, my family took a trip to see
my mother's brother Uncle Del and his family in St. Joseph,
Missouri. This was the trip to solidify the newly blended
family and for my mother to introduce her new husband
to her older brother. Her younger brother, Uncle Dick—
cursed with wanderlust all his life—had hit the rails again
for a hobo's life on the road and was supposed to meet us
there.

The trip to Missouri sounded rational and well thought
out, but I resented it. We would be gone for two weeks
because after St. Joe, we were to travel to Benton Harbor,
Michigan, for sun and fun on the shores of Lake Michigan.
I hated being pulled away from Terry and our adventures.

The trip seemed to last forever. My cousins on my mother's side were so much younger that I couldn't relate to them,
and my hormones were rising like the mercury in a midwest-
ern thermometer.

From Missouri, we headed to Michigan. By then, I felt
as though I'd been on the road a year. I couldn't wait to get
back to the sandbox. That was the first time in my life I
stayed in a motel. I was bored beyond belief, and my attitude
deteriorated. I'd spent too much time on the beach and had
gotten the worst sunburn of my life. I was in such pain that
I couldn't bend my legs. We went to a drive-in movie one
night, and I had to sit in the back seat with my legs straight
out, resting on the top of the front seat. Finally, after what

seemed like a thousand years, we went home.

When we got back to Fort Wayne, something had changed—not the sandbox; it was like I'd left it. Not Terry—he was still a goofy, good-natured kid. It was me. I wasn't a kid anymore, at least not in my mind. Almost overnight, *Mad* magazine made sense to me, grown-ups were to be avoided, and Elvis was the coolest guy on Earth. My body was quickly changing too. I grew my hair longer and started shaving the black fuzz on my upper lip. I began wearing my collar up like Elvis's. I heard the word *greaser* for the first time.

Having Chet around meant a new source of cigarettes. Instead of bumming smokes from my friends who swiped them from their parents, now I could provide an occasional pack. Chet smoked Spud cigarettes, the first mentholated brand in America, and I swiped them from the carton he kept in the bottom drawer of his dresser. Terry looked like a little boy to me now. His parents were together; his father lived at home. I still had a fantasy of my parents' getting back together even though Mom had married Chet. What the hell. She'd gotten one divorce; she could get another.

The darker the stubble on my lip grew, the more my mother and I fought. We fought over almost everything: my clothes, my curfew, my language, and, eventually, my smoking. One day, I walked out the door of the little neighborhood store where my friends and I hung out. There was my mother, and there I was—with a lit Lucky Strike hanging from my lips.

"Get home," she commanded. We met in the living room. "If you're going to smoke, you'll have to do it in front of me." She had tried child psychology before, and it hadn't worked. "Really?" I said, pulling my pack out of my shirt pocket and lighting up right there in the living room. "You smartass," she said and stomped off to the kitchen, which is where she went when she was mad at me.

I'd barely had time to adjust to my new reality when my father said he was going to marry a former high school friend who had one child, a daughter. Tim and I weren't invited to *his* wedding either. Now I had another stepsister and a whole bunch more step-cousins, step-uncles, step-aunts, even step-grandparents this time. Shortly after the wedding, my father and his wife had a baby girl they named Lynda, my half sister. My family was filled with strangers. Who were these people? Terry's family was sound, secure, normal, the model nuclear family. He wasn't a stepson. He had both legs. I dropped him as a friend almost overnight.

The one constant throughout that summer was going to the racetrack, but by the end of the season in September, I was sitting in the stands with the grown-ups more often. I was going into junior high now, seventh grade. The step-cousins would ask me to play tag, but I was interested in the races, I told them. I sat a little bit apart from the grown-ups. I mean, I had my pride. Anyway, Eddie Doyle was out there on the track now.

That's rookie of the year Eddie Doyle in the number 7 Ford coming up on the outside past Dick Salesman on the front straight. Something might be wrong with Salesman's car; he's slowing down! Doyle dives low into turn one, takes the inside groove, and tucks in behind Hook Henderson coming out of turn two. Doyle drag races Henderson down the back straight; Doyle goes low. Contact with Henderson. Henderson spins but keeps it on the track! It looks like there's some bad blood between Henderson and Doyle. Now Doyle is giving the chrome horn to Skeeter Grocock. He bumps him again! Doyle laughs as he passes Grocock. Doyle passes Cozy Coe on the outside. What a move! Now it's Doyle in front by one, two, three car lengths. The checker's out! Doyle wins! Ladies and gentlemen, this is his first feature win at South Anthony Speedway! What a driver! His beautiful girlfriend joins him in the winner's circle and showers him with kisses.

Everything I knew about racing, I learned from newsreels at the movies, TV, the grandstands at South Anthony Speedway, and the film The Big Wheel, starring Mickey Rooney. To see The Big Wheel now is to scratch your head in wonder. The director cut in footage from the 1949 Indianapolis 500, which had several wrecks. In one, a driver was thrown from his car, ran across the track, and got back into the cockpit. In the movie, a flaming accident on the last lap forces Billy Coy (Mickey Rooney) to drive through the inferno, setting his car on fire. He comes in third, with severely burned forearms. Bill Holland won the Borg Warner Trophy, but in the movie, he doesn't keep it. He gives it to Billy, which is pure Hollywood. No racecar driver would do such a thing. When I was a kid, though, I thought that was what racecar drivers were—brave, courageous, and generous. I also thought every racecar driver was rich.

2008-It's Only Money

Most local short track racing teams operate on shoestring budgets because racing is the original pay-to-play scheme. Almost no one makes money except the parts companies, oil companies, and manufacturers—and the track, of course. If the track doesn't make money, there's no track. In 2008, Stafford Motor Speedway charged $30 for a team car number and $185 for a NASCAR driver's license. A season pit pass was $410, and crewmembers paid for their own. Most crewmembers are friends. Todd Owen says about racing in general, "It's definitely a friendship thing." He says he likes to keep costs low because money changes drivers' characters. By that, he means the way they drive. It lowers their respect for other drivers. He admits that when he was racing a fully sponsored car, he "didn't mind taking off a couple of bumpers." He chuckles at the thought.

Just suiting up to drive is expensive. For a new racecar driver, the tab to drop the net and climb through the window is a little over $2,700. That includes the helmet, HANS device, fire suit, shoes, gloves, and flame retardant underwear and socks. Drivers can save money buying sale-priced or used gear, but why scrimp on safety or wear somebody's sweat-stained castoff? For the most part, this is a one-time-only cash outlay. Most drivers wear the same fire suit week after week. Some suits have that never-been-washed look. Fire? Some of them look as though they couldn't protect a driver from hot soup.

A winning driver earns 25 percent of the purse, and the owner gets the rest. In 2008, Stafford Motor Speedway paid $1,450 for a feature win, so the driver got $362.50 and the owner pocketed $1,087.50. Heat winners and consolation race winners got nothing. All the short tracks in Connecticut were in this price range. For a 20-week race schedule, the share for a driver who won every feature would be $7,250, but even the best drivers don't win every race. In fact, two drivers at one Connecticut track racked up four feature wins each for a total of $1,450 apiece if they had that 25 percent deal with the owner. If one of those four-time winning drivers was also the owner, he or she got to keep it all for a grand total of $5,800. Drivers got money for second and, at some tracks, third, but even winners could make more money mowing lawns from spring until fall.

Yes, drivers pay, but drivers who want to *own* their racecars pay even more. The basic car is everything except the motor and transmission. Drivers can save money buying used or building cars from scratch, as Todd Owen did, but still shell out $15,000 for a used ride and $20,000 for the built motor—$7,000 for a spec motor—and $1,000 to $1,600 for a typical Modified transmission. Todd's motor was rebuilt by engine builder Billy the Kid and will cost $16,000 to $17,000.

A typical team goes through one set of tires per week at $620 per set. The crew needs a pit box for those long feature races. That costs between $5,000 and $7,000, but it should last many seasons. A well-heeled owner might pay for the crew's season pit passes. A typical crew has seven members, so an owner needs to cough up $410 each for a total of $2,870. The car needs 15 gallons of 113 octane fuel at around $9 to $10 a gallon for just one night of racing in 2008, which includes practice, hot laps, heat races, and the feature. It cost $70 a week in fuel to get the car to the track on a fifth-wheel trailer hauled by a dually pickup. A good used trailer—the portable race shop—runs around $11,000. Add it all up, and the first season costs around $72,500—and that's if the driver doesn't total the car. A bad wreck can easily cause $25,000 worth of damage. Some owners make drivers sign a "no-wreck" clause that holds drivers financially responsible for accidents. I saw a Late Model race at Waterford in which one car tangled with another and hit the wall on the backstretch, destroying the front end. A track announcer interviewed the driver while the safety crew cleaned up the mess. "That's it," said the driver. "I'm finished racing for good. I signed a no-wreck clause, and I can't afford to fix it."

A wreck sends a car to a frame shop to have everything that's broken cut off, re-welded, and bent back to specifications. Unless there's a back-up car, the team works until midnight every night putting it together for next week's race. Renting the track to test repairs and setups could cost $1,500 for the whole day or $2,500 for four or five hours, depending on the track. These expenses are for local, short track, asphalt racing. Owning a NASCAR tour Modified and hauling it to tracks from state to state can easily double or triple the cost.

In 2008, contingency sponsors (the decals in front of the number) paid $450 for a first place feature win and $150 for second. The driver usually gets the money but, again, it depends on the deal with the owner. Sometimes the winning team gets free tires or other parts. An owner who has a top driver might lay out only $65,000 to run a full season the first year. There are regional differences. Most tracks in the South, West, and Midwest pay less in prize money, but expenses are lower. It's all relative—and expensive wherever it is. The bottom line is there is no bottom line. I eliminate one of my questions about what makes a racer race. It's not about the money.

Depending on the deal, the driver pays the bills, so the driver brings the sponsor, even at the highest levels of racing. It's up to the driver to pound the pavement with his or her presentation book and look for sponsorship money. Around New England, sponsors are a motorcycle dealer, the Indian casinos, a dentist, a milk company, car dealers, and other assorted community businesses. Todd Owen brought his employer, a construction company, to the car's owner. A full sponsor can pay $10,000 to put a logo on the hood, rear, or side of a local short track racecar, but it merely offsets some costs. There's still a giant deficit, but it keeps small performance-parts businesses, welding shops, tire dealers, distributors, and motor builders such as Billy the Kid in the black.

Motor Head

Billy the Kid's engine shop is a steel building tucked away in a mixed industrial neighborhood in Torrington, Connecticut. Inside, the smells of machine oil and cold iron hang in the air, perfume to the mechanically inclined. Tall green metal shelves store oil-stained boxes of parts, and on a long workbench, shiny, silvery engine blocks sit next to rusted brown hulks waiting to be cleaned, milled, and polished. This is a world of mechanical extremes, of heavy lifting and precision micrometric accuracy.

In Northeast short track racing, Billy the Kid builds many of the engines in the top divisions; there are few motors without his label. When I ask drivers in the pits what Billy the Kid's real name is, they don't know. They never call him anything else.

Billy "the Kid" Mathes is in constant motion in the pits, checking on his customers, who, like everyone else in local short track racing, are his friends. The Kid, dark curly hair flecked with gray, stocky and barrel-chested like one of his motors, grew up on a farm in Harwinton, Connecticut. "I was forced into repairing everything on the farm from tractors to chainsaws." He left the University of Connecticut and went to a trade school near his home, enrolling in the EPM program—electrical, power, mechanics.

In the back of the shop, a 2002 Corvette Z06 rests on a lift high over the floor. A big German shepherd named Bear follows us around as the Kid points out the different machines and explains the process of building a motor. His son, Curtis, works for him, and an older man sits in the parts room reading a newspaper. Wendy manages the small office off the shop floor.

The Kid's been in business for 25 years, although it started slowly right after he was married. He and his new wife agreed he would start his own business someday, and then the opportunity to buy a garage came along. Eventually, success came, and when his four children were born, he was able to pay cash for each hospital bill. One of his kids is studying to become a neurosurgeon. The Kid started with no money and built his business and his good name over time. He still works—"a double," he calls it—70 hours a week because he loves what he's doing. His focus on service in the pits the day of a race has forced other engine builders to do the same, which is difficult for out-of-state shops.

An affable man who looks me straight in the eye when he talks, the Kid has an affinity for motors. "I like to take a motor and make it run better than the factory. We were at Lime Rock for an engine test last Tuesday. They were turning times of 55 seconds and happy with it. I heard something wrong with the motor. I said 'Cup cars turn faster times than that.'" He looked, and sure enough, a spark plug wire on the number seven cylinder had come off. He put it back on, and the car turned a 54-second lap.

The Kid builds engines for street cars too but admits that as far as his business goes, the Whelen Modified Tour cars are the biggest piece of the pie financially. He says tour cars are "100 percent high quality," while with the local SK Modifieds, "everything is spec." Both motors start life as a basic Chevy 350 V-8 block. Several rusted blocks sitting on the shop floor are waiting to be rehabilitated. The Whelen block is bored out to 358 cubic inches, and the SK is 357 cubes, a slight but significant difference when combined with the other specifications. The tour Modified motor has an 18-degree valve angle; an SK has a 23-degree angle. The tour cars have small, four-barrel Holley carbs; the SKs have two barrels. The tour motor puts out 600 horses with a timing belt; the SK has 420 ponies with a timing chain. Both motors have "Snoopy chambers," named after Charlie Brown's dog. The Kid turns over a heavy cast-iron head to show that the top of the combustion chamber is shaped like a profile of Snoopy's head.

The Kid explains that the limit on Whelen Tour racecar motors is 427 cubic inches, but nobody runs it. It makes the car heavy and causes the tires to wear out too quickly. To keep power and weight balanced, he calculates 6.8 pounds of car per cubic inch of engine.

Not surprisingly, the Kid's no fan of sealed crate and spec motors, a trend that NASCAR and the local tracks are pursuing to keep costs down. "The minute you take the racer out of the racer, you've failed. It robs people of their creativity and competitive urges. There isn't a week that goes by that I don't have something new to try." He's not alone.

The Cars

Performance Racing Industry magazine estimated that worldwide, 385,000 racers competed in at least one race a year, and that's just the drivers. Racing is big business. The U.S. market alone was estimated at $13.5 billion in 2008, and that didn't include the behind-the-scenes engineering investment from people such as the Kid. The *PRI* annual trade show in Orlando, Florida, is one of the biggest in the world, with more than 1,200 companies from all 50 states and 67 countries on display.

Every state has oval short tracks paved with concrete, asphalt, or simply hard-packed dirt. Even Hawaii has two—along with four drag strips and a road course—and every short track in America has a hierarchy of racing divisions. It can be confusing to the casual fan because there's no national standard. In 2008, Connecticut didn't have a statewide standard, as Scott Foster Jr. pointed out. Every track had its own detailed rules for each of its divisions, which ranged from a few paragraphs to a booklet as thick as a small-town phone book.

I don't know anything about truck races or dirt tracks. I've never been to either, but I've seen them on TV. Trucks just don't interest me, and frankly, dirt Modifieds and Late Models are just plain ugly. They're big and boxy, riding high off the ground, the body angles sharp and unpleasant to look at. They look as if they were made of plywood sheets. My half sister, Lynda, and her family love dirt track racing. They speak fondly of sitting in the grandstands picking mud out of their hair at the end of the evening. I'll stick with pavement.

Racing divisions at a typical track start at the bottom with an entry-level car, such as a four-cylinder or V-8 powered former passenger car or a fiberglass replica powered by a motorcycle or kart motor. The former passenger cars go by different names, but they're easy to spot from the grandstand. Beat up, smashed up, sometimes just one sponsor or none, the cars look as though they won't make one lap around the track before fenders start falling off. However, the drivers are no less motivated to win than the Sprint Cup cowboys on Sunday afternoon at Daytona. This is the most affordable end of local short track racing.

At my tracks, the four-cylinder cars are called Mini Stocks. They're 1978 or newer, front engine, rear drive only, two-door coupes—doors welded shut and all glass removed—with motors no bigger than 2,400 cc's. The motors must be stock to the models.

Fiberglass Legends Cars are built entirely for racing. They've never spent a day on the street. No teenaged lovers ever lost their virginity in one of these. Legends are 5/8 scale fiberglass replicas of the chopped-down 1934 to 1940 Chevy, Dodge, and Ford coupes and sedans similar in exterior looks to the ones that raced at South Anthony Speedway, only smaller. Yamaha motorcycle engines power these cars. Legends Cars generally look to be in good shape because the bodies don't dent, and cracks or holes are easy to repair.

The Bandolero is powered by a Briggs & Stratton kart motor and is an even smaller and lighter entry-level race-car, but the fiberglass body resembles modern Toyota and Honda sedans.

On the next rung up the competition ladder are former

A Legend car on display at a pit party in the infield at Waterford Speedbowl.

V-8 street cars called Hobby Stocks, Limited Sportsmen, Bomber Cars, Thunder Cars, or, at one of my tracks, DARE Stocks after the elementary school antidrug program. If you've ever wondered what happened to that 1985 Buick Regal your dad used to own, here it is. The cars are 108-inch-wheelbase, 1980s Chevy Malibus, Monte Carlos, Buick Regal V-8's, and similar models. Like the Mini Stocks, the Hobby Stocks have been modified: doors welded shut, glass removed, tubular roll cages to protect the drivers and special racing gas tanks installed. Everyone at the track races on the same tires, usually Hoosier, but they can be Goodyear too.

The next level is a little more complicated and expensive, depending on the track. Two branches go in different directions: open-wheeled and full-fendered. Each of my local tracks has an entry-level division for open-wheeled Modified racing. At Thompson, they're called Thompson Modifieds.

Todd Owen's SK Modified sits on a jack in the pits at Stafford Motor Speedway.

X Modifieds race at the Speedbowl, and SK Light Modifieds are based at Stafford. The SK Lights and all the other entry-level Mods run factory-sealed Circle Track 350 V-8 crate motors or something similar. At Thompson, it's a Jasper 355 or a GM ZZ4. No tinkering allowed with these motors. A team that breaks the seal is disqualified. The cars look similar to the top-of-the-heap Modifieds but generally have less sponsorship and are cheaper to run for the season than full Modifieds. There are a lot more wrecks in all these entry-level divisions because the drivers haven't honed their skills yet or have gone as far as they can with the talent they have.

Woody Pitkat's Late Model makes his way through lapped traffic at Stafford Motor Speedway.

Regulations for full-fendered models depend on the track. At Stafford, the Limited Late Model looks like a Late Model, but it doesn't have a Lexan spoiler on the rear trunk lid. The 350 horsepower engine is a built motor, which means it's not a crate motor—it can be worked on—but it has cheaper components than the Late Model in the next jump up.

At most tracks, Late Models are at the top of the heap in full-fendered racing. Late Models and Limited Late Models are built from the ground up for racing. The bodies are usually polyplastic front and rear with sheet metal side panels. The bodies are made by racing manufacturers and are supposed to resemble the Chevy Lumina, Monte Carlo, Pontiac Grand Prix, and other street cars of that type.

A typical Late Model weighs 3,100 pounds with the driver and has a wheelbase of 108 inches. A 400-horsepower, 350-cubic-inch Chevy, 351-cubic-inch Ford, or 360-cubic-inch Mopar motor with a Holley two-barrel carburetor sucks in air and gasoline at the rate of 1 gallon per 5 miles. Thompson goes one notch higher with its Pro

Stock division, or Super Late Model—2,900 pounds with driver, 358-cubic-inch motor with a four-barrel carb, 104-inch wheelbase riding on 10-inch slicks, the same tire the Modifieds use.

The Modifieds are the fastest, deadliest, and, to most fans, sexiest cars on the track. They use the same motors as Late Models or Pro Stocks, but the internal components

Whelen Modified Tour cars go through inspection at New Hampshire Motor Speedway. They're checked for several specifications, including height of car, weight and ground clearance. (Pat McGrath photo)

boost the horsepower to 425, even with a two-barrel carb. These cars are weighed with the driver and must tip the scales at 2,600 pounds or more.

The top divisions at my tracks—Modified, Pro Stock, and Late Model—have two-way radios between drivers and spotters. Limited Late Models, Street Stocks, Mini Stocks, Legends, and Bandoleros do not. Those cars have one-way radios and can transmit only instructions from the race director. The drivers are on their own when they want to pass.

My tracks require the attachment of transponders to the car frames in all divisions to keep count of laps run.

Touring classes are different from but similar to the locals'. Tour racers live on the road, driving all over the Northeast, South, West, and Midwest. They visit tracks and bring their own prize money, rules, starters, PA announcers, race directors, and other officials. The cars are all heavily sponsored and look fresh from the showroom floor. An official for the Northeast Midget Association calls its bunch a traveling circus.

A hierarchy similar to the local tracks' applies to the traveling series. In the Northeast, there's an entry-level series called Pro-4 Modifieds. They're open-wheeled and low cost, relatively speaking. Any four-cylinder motor up to 2,330 cubic centimeters is allowed as long as it's not a rotary type.

The fastest cars on tour in the Northeast are the big-block Supermodifieds from the International Supermodified Association. Their motto is "Balls to the wall, hangin' to the left." The motor is a 470-cubic-inch, 700-horsepower Chevy V-8 mounted off-center to the inside left of the car. It slurps methanol through four two-barrel carburetors. The motor's weight on the inside left and a 24-square-foot wing on top keep the car on the track as it approaches the turns at 178 miles an hour on a 5/8 mile oval. Air shocks control the wing's angle. The wing flattens out at high speed on the straights and tips forward and down when the car slows, keeping it pressed to the track through the turns. The body and the wing are aluminum, making the car relatively light at 2,050 pounds with the driver. These cars have direct drive (no transmission), and they need to be push started like the Midgets. Even though they have rudimentary mufflers, I have to wear ear protection when these cars are on the track. Watching that wing change position, seemingly with a mind of its own as the car flies around the speedway, is

Winged Midgets in turn four at Waterford Speedbowl. Erica Santos in the #44 follows closely behind Randy Cabral in the #47.

spooky; the driver has no direct control. The air shocks are charged before the race, according to the size of the track.

The Supermodified's pint-sized cousin is the winged Midget from the Northeast Midget Association and the wingless counterpart from the United States Auto Club. A typical Midget weighs only 850 to 925 pounds without the driver, depending on the type of engine, and has a 68- to 76-inch wheelbase. The cars have mostly four-cylinder VW, Chevy, Esslinger, Cosworth, Mopar, or Race Tek motors. A small Chevy V-6 is allowed. Honda recently jumped into the market with a four-banger. As with the Supermods, drivers have one-way radios to get instructions from the race director, and the cars run on methanol, have direct drive, and have to be push started. However, the wings on Midgets are fixed and don't change angles during a race.

The NASCAR Grand National regional touring cars look almost exactly like the Sprint Cup cars that NASCAR races every Sunday. The Grand National motor is a spec engine built by Wegner Automotive Research. It's V-8 motor, four-barrel carb, putting out 625 horses at 8,000 rpm. The motor is available as a kit or fully assembled. It's not sealed but has to be freshened or repaired with approved parts only.

Other tour groups race at my local tracks, such as the Pro All Stars Series and the American-Canadian Tour. The cars are essentially Pro Stocks and Super Late Models, and the groups provide their own personnel and prize money.

The oldest short track touring group in NASCAR is the Whelen Modified Tour, formerly the Featherlite Tour. Whelen Mods look similar to SK Mods, but all the parts are the best money can buy, particularly in the power plant.

The internal differences in the motor are reflected in the costs. Rods in an SK car are $600; in a Whelen car, they're $1,800. An SK motor costs $15,000, and a Whelen motor costs $44,000.

Some of the richer Whelen teams haul their cars with combination tractor-trailers/motor homes called toters. They are hooked to trailers the size of moving vans and can haul four racecars and a fully functioning race shop. An entry-level DARE Stock team at a local track can run a season for maybe $15,000. The Whelen season will cost $150,000 or more to run full-time.

Car counts rise and fall in all divisions according to an area's economy and how well managed the track is. One of my local tracks, the Waterford Speedbowl, manages to attract a small but loyal group of racers and fans even though it's been on the verge of collapse for years. The other two—Thompson and Stafford—do well enough to stay out of trouble even in bad economic times and 2008 was the beginning of some very bad economic times indeed.

All these specs and divisions can change with the end of

a season as rules are modified and sponsors come and go, but what endures is the system that brings drivers along and keeps racing competitive and fun to do and watch. And it's up to track officials to maintain order.

Drivers' Meeting

In the Stafford Motor Speedway paddock, July 25, 2008:

"Welcome to the CarQuest 150 for the SKs. I want to thank, uh, everybody for coming tonight. We have a great turnout for SKs for this 150. We want to start the meeting off and tell you that, uh, last week, all the divisions, the starts and re-starts were starting to get a little ragged. Guys—and girls—I know you guys understand where we want to go and what we want to do. We do not want to get back into the, the rhythm where we're starting early and playing games. It's an easy transition. Once you come out of turn four, you have to be between the cones. And Bo Gunning, who starts the race? There you go. The starter starts the race. So, uh, you know we've been putting people back. We put a couple people back last week. We put some back the week before for jumping the starts. It's an easy thing for us to do. It's very hard for you guys to make that up in the time that you have, so, uh, put us in the situation, and we're going to make that call. You need—excuse me? OK, when you jump, we'll do it before we go green. We'll just tell you to go to the back because you have enough laps, Gary. All right, but uh, all kidding aside, uh, it's real easy to do. It's been working out very well as far as getting into turn one. Everybody understands what I mean, so, uh, we're going to continue to do what we been doing as far as starts and restarts, but you cannot play the game. You have to do it together.

"Guys, uh, 150 laps for the SKs. Yellow laps do count. If you're in the pit area and laps are clicking off, you are going down laps. Absolutely. Go down laps to the field. Lucky dog—if you are the highest running car down one lap, we do have the lucky dog. We will let you pass the pace car and get back on the lead lap if we go yellow, but you need to remember something. If you're the lucky dog, you cannot go in the pits. You have to wait until we tell you to drive around the pace car. By that time, it'll be one to go. So, uh, we don't allow you to pit if you're the lucky dog. If you do pit, you're not the lucky dog.

"If you spin out on the racetrack and you sit there, a situation where we feel as though you can get going, and we need to go yellow, you're going automatically down a lap, automatically down a lap in all divisions if you sit on the racetrack. If there's a rough riding call against you, you do not go down a lap. If somebody spins you or whatever the situation is, or if you spin in front of the field and we feel as though it's a dangerous situation, we go yellow fast, you will not go down a lap. It's at the discretion of race control.

"We're starting 30 cars tonight for the SKs, and as of right now, I'm going to run two consis. Two consis for the SKs. I'm going to split them up. Lapped cars. You need to know if you're getting lapped, we want you to the bottom of the racetrack. Let the leaders know you're going to be on the bottom. Give them a lead to drive around you. If you're not up to racing speed, we're going to black flag you and tell you have to get up to racing speed. We will let you out one time. If you don't get up to racing speed, we're going to park you for the night. With ten laps to go, any lapped cars in the top ten, we take you out. We put the lapped cars starting eleventh back, the top ten cars will, uh, get a chance to, uh, finish the race with no lapped cars in the way.

"One quick thing—when you guys line up for warm-ups, I want to see two rows in the back. I don't want to see you scattered all over the place. Two rows. The person on the third turn gate will let a row go at a time, so, uh, just get in a row when it's time for your warm-ups. Do not make a mess of the back paddock area. Keep it tight to the fence.

"We'd like to see all drivers—all drivers—stay with their racecars if you get in a wreck. Stay with your racecar. If a driver leaves the scene, we're just going to tow his car out the turn three gate, and we're just going to drop it there. And if he needs help loading it with a wrecker, it won't happen till the very end of the night, and if you need, and if you make contact with the wall, if you make contact with the wall or another driver, and it needs to be towed, we want the driver to be seen by EMR. That's fine. No problem. If you get a flat tire and want to be towed in, no problem. If you make contact with a car that has damage—I'm talking *damage*, absolutely, no problem. If you think you can get your car fixed and you're being towed in with either, with a flat, or like Terry said, you're dragging something and you want to be towed, you can stay in the car or with the car, but if you make heavy contact with another car or the wall, I want you to go to EMR.

"For the Lights, the Limiteds, and the Dare Stocks, we have a situation where if you come down pit road, you're done with your feature. We don't let you back out. What we're going to do is, if it's a safety situation where you think either you're leaking something or you're not sure you're getting a flat tire or something, if you come down pit road, we want you stop where Chuck Sitowski is. He's on that little tower in the infield. If you ask him a question as far as safety, is my car OK? And he says yes, you can go back out, but if you have to work on the car or anybody touches the car, pulls a fender—anything—you cannot go back out. Only for a safety situation. If you think you're getting a flat or some situation like that, do I have a bent tie rod? Is my front tire pointing towards Mars? Or something, you know, under those situations we will let you back out.

"Outside intros for the SK drivers tonight. As of right now, if it changes, we'll let you know, but we want you to grid up in your starting position on the mini-mile like we did for the Sizzler. Autograph sessions for the SKs right after your heats. Right out the door here, right out the gate. SK drivers, autograph session right after your heats.

"And on a lighter note, we got a couple e-mails about drivers showing displeasure with other drivers this week. Guys, I just want to let youse know, you know, I understand the passion, the fire that burns, but if you want to give somebody the finger, do it in turns two or three, don't do it down the front stretch, OK? No problem. All right, drivers. Late Models, get 'em lined up. Late Models, get 'em lined up."

The Two Mr. Assholes

Mark Arute, co-owner of Stafford Motor Speedway, hired John Johnson and Jay Shea to be the tech directors at the track because of the old adage: it takes a thief to catch a thief. "Well, we did have the reputation for being the biggest cheaters around," says John with a wide smile. "That's how we got hired. We used to be called assholes. Now, it's Mr. Assholes."

Jay, 32, is John's son-in-law and was the crew chief for the pair's Late Model team. John, 62, was the driver. They did well at regional tracks even with a small, four-person crew. Some of the teams had 20 crewmembers. Although John and Jay never won a championship, they had the fastest car at Thompson International Speedway. "Two years in a row, we finished second in points to a guy we knew was illegal," says Jay. "But he was best friends with the tech officials, and when we would win, they'd pull crankshafts, heads, everything. When he would win, they'd pull carburetors. To be honest with you, that was the main reason we became officials. We told Mark we wanted to treat people the way we wish we were treated when we raced."

John's racing career came to an abrupt end on a street in Agawam, Massachusetts, when a woman ran an intersection and T-boned his pickup at 40 miles per hour. "They told me not to get back in a racecar if I wanted to use my arms. I've got plates and screws in my neck. My neck is bad." In all his years of competing, he was never hurt. He even hit the wall hard a couple of times. When asked about the allure of racing, he doesn't hesitate. "Speed. Speed. It's the only place I relaxed."

John's story isn't typical among racecar drivers. When he and his late wife, Crystal, were first married, the couple had a '58 Chevy convertible that they raced at drag strips. It had fat rear tires and three two-barrel carbs parked on top of a 348-cubic-inch engine. Their family car was a racecar. When a baby came along, Crystal said it was time to get a real car, so they sold the Chevy and bought a Rambler. As their family grew, John and Crystal went to the races as spectators. One day, a friend asked John to help him build a racecar. They took it to a local track to race, and his friend—the driver—never even qualified. "He would back off; he had no guts. My wife says, 'Why don't you build your own racecar? The kids are all grown.'" So, in his early 40s, John started his career as a racecar driver.

Crystal drove Midgets when she was a kid, but her father said a woman wasn't supposed to drive a racecar, so she quit. However, her desire remained. "Soon as we started the racecar up in the garage, she come flying out and smelled the fuel," says John. "It's got an aroma to it that just sparks you."

The Johnson Late Model team cheated any way it could. One night, the crew took the right rear brake shoes off and put a ball bearing in the brake line to stop the flow of brake fluid to the right rear wheel. When the car went around the turns, the fully functioning left rear brake helped pull the car around, allowing for more speed. In inspection, the tech officials simply pulled the brake line and if fluid ran out, the team had a win. The officials caught the Johnson team. "They told us don't come back unless the brake shoes are on the car," says Jay. For the next week's race, "We took the brake shoes and welded them to the trunk lid."

They explain that the rulebook was vague back then and that their job as competitors was to twist it to their advantage. In one race, they won using a carbon fiber clutch plate. The rules said no aluminum clutch plates and after inspection, the officials said they were DQ'd. John and Jay asked why and were told that the clutch plate wasn't steel. There's a little lawyer in every race team, and a smart crew will learn to read between the lines of the rulebook. Jay said, "It doesn't say steel in the rule book. It just says 'must not be aluminum centers.' It doesn't say it has to be a steel center." The officials huddled and admitted the team was right. One official said, "You got your win, but Monday morning, the rule will be changed."

Their Late Model was shortened, lengthened, and widened by using a Canadian chassis. Every junkyard has a giant parts book that lists the numbers of American car chassis that can be used for racing under the rules. There were no numbers for Canadian chassis. That chassis today sits in a garage in Agawam as a collector's item. The man who owns it today says he'll never cut it up because "any idiots who shortened, lengthened, and widened a car, and you can't find it, I'm going to keep the chassis."

The trick at the track was to stay one step ahead of the inspectors. One week, the Johnson team modified the rear end by having a special axle made that offset the car to the left. They moved the body over on the frame so it wouldn't be noticed. They'd run the car like that for two weeks until another team caught on and complained to the officials. Before the next race, John and Jay would pull off the rear end and put the body back where it belonged. The inspectors had been alerted, and they wanted to measure the car. Three or four weeks after the car passed, John and Jay would put their custom rear end back on.

Left-side weight is important in an oval track racecar, and every division has rules about left-right weight distribution. A driver John and Jay knew hid a heavy lead weight controlled by a cable where inspectors never looked—under the dash. During the race, he'd draw the weight from the right side to the left side of the car. "When he was out there racing, the car was a rocket ship," says Jay. When the driver took his car through inspection, he'd slide the weight back to the right side before he drove onto the scale.

Another trick John and Jay used was to pipe in the overflow. A racecar has an overflow tank to catch superheated water escaping from the radiator so that it doesn't run onto the track. John and Jay would direct the hose that connected the tank into the hollow-tube frame's left side. As the water came out of the radiator, it filled the left side of the frame, making it heavier and the car faster. After the race, if they were to go through inspection, one of the crewmembers would go over before the car got on the scale and tell the inspector, "I'm just draining the pet [petcock valve]." In fact, he was draining the frame.

The team found another way to cheat at the now-closed Riverside Speedway, which used to be on the banks of the Connecticut River in Agawam, Massachusetts. "This one night, we tried this new tire softener. Well, don't I get a flat tire." His crewmembers saw the inspectors walking toward their pit stall, so one of the crew threw the tire into the river. "You wouldn't believe the smell that came off that tire." Speaking of tires, another way to cheat was to slice the tire code off a legal tire and glue it to an illegal tire.

Jay leans forward in his chair, enjoying another memory. "One time, we tried to run propylene oxide, which is jet fuel. You mix it in the fuel tank. The only problem is you have to park way out in the middle of nowhere 'cause it stinks. John started sixth. He was first by a half a lap, and I'm thinking if we don't get caught, this is going to be cool. All of a sudden, three laps later, you hear all this popping, and the car comes to a stop. No one ever told me you have to change all the rubber gaskets in the carburetor to brass because eventually the propylene oxide eats them up. We would've won that race by a lap."

All divisions have rules and ways to get around them. A locked differential is allowed in Late Models but not in Limited Late Models, the division one notch below. A family car has a limited slip differential, so when it goes around a corner, the inside wheel goes slower; otherwise, if the axle were locked, the inside wheel would spin faster and wear off the rubber on the tires. In Limited Late Models, the rulebook requires this stock kind of axle, mainly to keep expenses down. John and Jay busted one Limited Late Model team for having shims in the axle. The shims are normal when they're cool, but as the race goes on, they heat up, expand, and lock the rear axles, allowing both wheels to turn at the same time, which gives the car more speed through the corners.

John and Jay have a system as inspectors. They don't tell anybody what they're going to inspect. They don't trust even other officials because they might be friends with teams and could slip and say something, giving advance notice of what would be checked that night. John and Jay keep a log of every teardown on each car so they can inspect different parts every time. Jay says they also go easy on the racers who never run up front if they should happen to win a race. "We say to ourselves, let's do something simple so this guy can go home." The pair wanders through the pits before a race, spot-checking cars. When they find a violation, they tell the team that should they win, the car won't pass. Usually, by the following week, the errant team will have fixed the problem, but they agree that they can't catch everything.

One year, John and Jay cost a driver the championship in Modified Lights. They had decided to do something simple and just check the brake calipers. The top three cars in points were illegal. Shelly Perry was fourth in the race, but she was third in points for the season. She had already loaded her car and was sitting in the grandstands, but they knew there would be a big controversy if they awarded the race to Shelly without checking her car. They had to hunt for her, and the first thing they did was ask her if her calipers were OK. She said, "You want to know something? I changed them last week. I had a feeling that's where you guys were going to go." They took her car off the trailer and checked her brakes. She won the championship.

The biggest violation they ever caught was an illegal frame bent to an extreme offset. The driver's excuse was that his grandmother owned the car and had hit a tree. He built his racecar on top of the frame and didn't know it was bent that much. John said to the driver, "Do you really think we're going to believe that?"

John and Jay have been technical inspectors at Stafford since 1998. The track pays John a fee, but Jay is a volunteer. Track management never argues about their decisions, and their word is final. The track just wants to know who is disqualified so the officials aren't caught off guard. Despite their roles, John and Jay have good relationships with the race teams. They camp at the track and used to go to parties with the teams after the races, but now they try to stay away from socializing because of controversy, rumors, and perception. They're friends with a couple of other officials, so they have their own little clique. They might go to a few parties, but they tend to keep to themselves. Says John, "We try to be as fair as we can, but don't cross that line because it don't matter who you are, you're going to get DQ'd."

They learned an important lesson when they were racing. "Over the years, we learned the less cheating you do, the faster you go," says John.

Every year, the track sends them to parts shows and NASCAR seminars on cheating. Even in Sprint Cup, left-side weight transfer is a popular flimflam. "And you think we cheat? These guys are horrible," says John. "I mean, fire extinguishers that weigh 60 pounds with nothing in them except lead. They had a radio that weighed 67 pounds." Says Jay, "If it weren't for cheating, Richard Petty wouldn't even be close to 200 wins."

John admits, "The cheating part is the fun part. It's trying to beat the officials. It's still fun. It's their job to cheat and our job to catch them. It's a game. We only got caught three times in all those years we were racing."

Illegal parts for sale on the open market are common now; in fact, John says, it's the number one excuse when a driver is caught: "I bought it that way." The parts are manufactured just for getting around the rules and are on display at the annual *Performance Racing Industry* magazine trade show in Orlando. John and Jay say that Brzezinski Racing Products is the worst offender. "Brzezinski hides when he sees us coming." The company's website leaves barely any doubt:

> "Looking for a winning set of heads or an intake manifold that will set you apart from the competition? Want that 'UnderCover Advantage' that leaves your competitors scratching their heads? You have come to the right place."

John explains that playing mind games is a big part of cheating. One time, John took several old-fashioned school desks—the kind with the chair attached to the desk—to the track. When the tech officials came by his pits to take measurements and make their pronouncements, John and his crew unloaded the desks and placed them in rows in front of the officials, creating an outdoor classroom. The crew taped notes under the car that said things such as "You're looking in the wrong place" or "Not here."

At another track, no radios were allowed in the cars, so Jay welded a radio antenna to the roof. Every week, the officials would search the car for the radio and miss the illegal parts everywhere else. The officials would ask them why they were using an antenna. "Uh, the TV gets better reception."

John and Jay tell the drivers three things to do to make a winning racecar, and they have nothing to do with cheating.

1. Communicate with the crew chief: the driver has to articulate what the car needs to make it stick to the track, and the crew chief has to be able to make the adjustments.

2. Maintain the car: "I used to pull that car apart every week and reassemble it, and I'd always find something small that was wrong," says Jay.

3. Make sure everything's in place: motor, transmission, rear end, and chassis.

Jay looks at his hands. "It took us a long time to find the right combination. Once we went 100 percent legal, we were faster."

John and Jay do a thorough inspection after the races, which usually end around 10 or 10:30 at night. Sometimes they're there until 2 a.m., inspecting the winning cars. "What nobody realizes is that the guys that run up front are legal 'cause we tech them all the time. The guys in the back are probably not legal 'cause they never finish up front, and we never check them. Our feeling is if you're not up front— except for safety—why do we need to worry about you?"

Both men sing the praises of Ted Christopher. "He's a

great driver, and we can tell you with no doubt in our minds that TC's cars are always legal. If we tell you that the rules are everybody's left-side weight is 55 percent, most will be 53.9, things like that. TC comes in; he's almost exactly at 55. Everything is right to the edge. The biggest thing TC does, from lap to lap, the car does not lose speed. The car stays the same. With everybody else, the cars slow down so it appears that TC is going faster, but he's not. They keep that car from lap one to lap 40 perfect where everybody else keeps dropping off."

John has been watching Ted closely for many years. "If you watch TC, he hits every mark. That mark is the point of no return. A good driver told me once, take it in until it breaks loose, wants to come around. That's where you stop, and that's how you learn to drive it. If you notice, TC takes it to that point, gets on the brakes, lets the car drop, lets the car drift a little bit, then gets back on the fuel. So he's actually slowed down more than anybody else in the turn but gets back on the fuel quicker." John explains that TC also has had the same sharp crew at Stafford for a long time. They set up everything he drives there, and they know how he drives it. "You have to have a lot of faith in your spotters and tires. That's why we got fast. My other son-in-law was my tire guy and my spotter, and if he said go low, I didn't look in my mirror. I went low," says John.

Although they're not racing now, John Johnson and Jay Shea love what they're doing. John gives me that wide smile again. "It's in the blood."

They agree that safety starts on day one. "When we do our inspection before we start practice on the first opening day, those cars have to go through a safety inspection every time. They have to come see us, or they can't go on the track. The seatbelts, the helmets—we have a whole list—gloves, fire suits, bars in the car, lead weights, make sure they're bolted on, everything is tight so it doesn't bounce around in the car, head rests—for every car in every division. We put a safety sticker on the car, and the guy that's running the back gate will let any car with a sticker on the track. If there's no sticker, he calls us."

OK, the cars and drivers are as safe as can be expected in an unsafe sport, but what about the track?

Indy East

On August 16, 2007, less than eight months before Shane Hammond's death, Modified drivers John Blewett III and his brother, Jimmy, were battling for the lead in the New England Dodge Dealers 150 at Thompson International Speedway. Witnesses said their cars were rubbing, shoving, brother on brother at 145 miles an hour. Jimmy went low and passed John when a wreck happened back in the pack. After a restart on lap 89, the brothers traded hard contact in turn four on lap 90. John tucked in behind Jimmy. On lap 93, John went below Jimmy in turn two for the lead, but Jimmy trailer-hitched him and passed him in turn four. John passed his brother again, and the caution flag flew because of a spin in the back of the pack. They restarted on lap 98, and Jimmy vaulted to the front in time to slow for another caution on lap 100. The green flag waved on lap 107, Jimmy got sideways in turn four and corrected it, and the two brothers crisscrossed as they flew past the flag stand, Woody Pitkat right behind in third. John went low into turn one. Jimmy got loose, their wheels touched, and Jimmy's car went airborne, landing on top of his brother's. Woody plowed into the tangled wreckage, and the red flag came out.

Jimmy dropped the net, climbed out of his car right away, looked into the cockpit of John's car, and began jumping up and down. The people in the press box laughed because they thought he was hopping mad at his brother for wrecking him. They couldn't see what Jimmy saw, the horror, the broken, jagged bumper bar from Jimmy's car piercing the sheet-metal roof, piercing John's helmet.

The drivers in the other cars shut off their motors. The crowd became eerily silent as the spectators realized what had happened—8,000 people holding their breath. The only sound came from the generators behind the food and souvenir stands on the midway. The drivers got out of their cars and gathered in the infield near the bottom of the turn. Four state police cruisers were parked near the accident, along with an ambulance, two wreckers, and a fire truck. It took 24 minutes to remove John, unconscious, his body still pumping adrenalin, clinging to life. Minutes later, when the ambulance slowly drove away, the crowd knew John was gone.

The race was suspended at 107 laps. John's stunned family loaded the broken car so it could be hauled back to the Blewett auto-wrecking yard in New Jersey. After the funeral, the family removed any reusable parts and crushed the car into a cube. No one could bear to look at it.

Another day—August 9, 2004. The New England Dodge Dealers 150, Thompson International Speedway. Rain had fallen on and off all afternoon. Finally, after a two-hour rain delay, the Modified feature race started. Driver Tommy Baldwin tried to avoid a multicar pile-up, swerved, and was hit from behind by Ronnie Silk. Baldwin's car careered into the wet infield grass; slid sideways, without slowing down; and hit three cement blocks guarding a light pole. He had to be cut from the car and died later at an area hospital.

July 19, 1987. Thompson. Corky Cookman, a top-ten NASCAR Modified driver, died when his throttle stuck in turn three and the car hit the wall almost head-on.

Once called "the Indianapolis of the East," Thompson was, and still is, the biggest, fastest, deadliest oval track in Connecticut. More racers have died at Thompson—12 drivers and one mechanic—than at any other track in the state. Only the road course at Lime Rock is close, at 11. Neither track comes close to matching Indy, though—68 drivers have died at the Indianapolis Motor Speedway. The Whelen Tour speed record at Thompson is 122.080 mph. Compare that to another legendary racetrack, the Bowman Gray Stadium bullring in North Carolina. The speed record there is about half what it is at Thompson, 68.254 mph.

In 1972, when he was 47 years old, Paul Newman drove in his first race at Thompson. Geoff Bodine and Tony Stewart raced there too. Three Thompson regulars in the 1940s went on to win the Indy 500: Mauri Rose, Bill Holland, and Lee Wallard. The first driver to die in a wreck at Thompson was Tony Willman, in a 1941 Midget race. Thompson was a charter member track of NASCAR and is still sanctioned today, as are all the Connecticut tracks.

The track and the racers try to make things safer after every fatality. After John Blewett III was killed, drivers reinforced their roofs and changed the bumper design and the brain bar. After Tommy Baldwin's death, the track redesigned the light poles in the infield and raised them onto a berm out of harm's way. When Corky Cookman died, the racers and builders redesigned the car frame so it would absorb the force of a hard impact without passing it to the driver.

I read about the Blewett, Baldwin, and Cookman fatalities in the newspaper. I wasn't there. The irony of the Blewett wreck was overwhelming: two brothers crash, one dies. The big brother who taught the little brother how to be a racecar driver is killed instantly.

After Shane Hammond's accident, fans were understandably looking at the safety of Thompson, questioning the lack of soft walls and catch fences in the turns and the wisdom of placing a rigid sign close to the track. Thompson has worked with the Connecticut Department of Motor Vehicles and the State Police to make the track safe. People die at Thompson International Speedway because it's big and fast. Winged Supermodifieds can hit more than 170 miles per hour going into the turns. It's the fastest track the Northeast Midget Association races. Driver Randy Cabral says, "This track scares me."

No racetrack is safe. Even the concept of an "accident" is suspect. A 2,600-pound car hurtles forward at 145 miles an hour, only inches from another car. The cars bang into each other, pushing, shoving, and dive-bombing in the corners on the outside edge of control. Something is bound to happen—a wreck? Certainly. How is that an accident?

In 1938, after visiting Winchester Speedway in Winchester, Indiana—a track still in business today—John Hoenig built a 5/8-mile paved oval on his dairy farm in the northeastern corner of Connecticut, just outside the picturesque, calendar-ready New England village of Thompson. It was the first paved racetrack in the country. John's son owns the track today.

Don Hoenig has a full head of white hair and the ruddy complexion of a man who has spent a lot of time on the golf course. In 2008, he shot his age—76. He designed and owns Raceway Golf Course, across the road from the track, and was inducted into the Connecticut Golf Hall of Fame in 1981.

Don speaks with a slight Boston–Rhode Island accent

and remembers when his father built the track. "He made his own pavement here. He took the stone walls from the farm, had a stone crusher crush the stones, and made all the mix right here. It wasn't hot tar; it was a cold mix 8 inches thick on the track. I remember the wooden grandstands being built." Back then—in addition to the oval track—a road course wound through the woods and through where part of the parking lot is today.

As a young man, Don did a little bit of everything at the track, from working the concession stands to cleaning the restrooms. He left home to attend the Rhode Island School of Design until he was drafted, ultimately serving in the Air Force. After the service, he became a golf professional and started designing and building golf courses. "I had my own construction outfit. I built like seven golf courses." His aging father asked him to come back and run the track, so Don bought the property from his father and aunt in 1964 and became deeply involved in the operation. The Sports Car Club of America found out about the track, and with its encouragement, Don redesigned the road course and ran amateur races on it until 1979. Paul Newman wasn't the only celeb who raced there in those days; so did Dave Garroway, Skitch Henderson, and Jackie Cooper. Because the racers were amateurs, there were no purses, just trophies. "It was a playground for them," says Don.

Then the track started to change. Professional road racing took over. Once, 200 to 300 cars would show up on a weekend and pay Don $125 each for the day to race. To bring in Trans Am and Can Am racing, he had to shell out $50,000 to $70,000. The TV stars Tommy and Dickie Smothers raced Can Am. "They'd sit in the kitchen, and my mother would make them some food." As the professional racers took over, the amateur racers felt pushed aside and were in no mood to help around the track for free.

"We were having problems because I had two- and three-day road course race events at the same time I was starting the NASCAR oval track every Sunday afternoon and evening. Two different kinds of people. Road course people were here to party. Then came the stock car people, and the two groups didn't really mix. There were a number of internal problems, so I closed the road course."

When touring groups such as the Northeast Midget Association, International Supermodified Association, Whelen Modified Tour, American Canadian Tour, and others are booked for a race, the track pays them a fee and then sets admission prices accordingly in order to make a profit. The Whelan Tour brings its own scales and tech headquarters in a large semi. Don always does a NASCAR program with the Midgets because NEMA, like most touring groups, is not NASCAR sanctioned. "I have to give them a guaranteed purse and get a separate insurance policy from a different company than NASCAR. NASCAR won't, never has, sanctioned Midget cars. Supermodifieds are the same; those are separate additions to enhance our show."

A Whelen Modified Tour 150-lap race costs Don about $70,000. Midgets add another $6,500. "It's cheaper, but the problem is they don't really have a fan base anymore."

That wasn't always the case. Midgets have been running since before World War II, mostly indoors. After the war and five long years without racing, Midget popularity exploded, especially in New England. A number of tracks were built. "They called it the Big Seven and the Little Seven," Don says. "They raced seven nights a week for Midgets, and on Sundays, they would have two races. Some guys had three or four cars. One guy had five Midgets called the Five Little Pigs. That was the Midget era. It went pretty good until the 1950s. Then in came stock car racing."

Thompson was one of the first tracks to run stock cars

before NASCAR came on the scene. Two local promoters organized a group they named United Auto Racers and called their cars Grand American cars: Fords, Chevys, Oldsmobile 88s, Hudson Hornets, and Studebakers. Then NASCAR took over and changed the name to Grand National. "They copied the little guy," says Don.

Don says the secret to running a racetrack is to know the clientele: where they come from, who they are, and which market best suits the track. Technology today allows tracks to identify their fans. He compares running a track to running a golf course. "You gotta know your people. Nothing against northern people; if you go to Maine, Vermont, New Hampshire, it's a different clientele than the NASCAR fan that comes here. We get white collar."

Thompson is a power track, which means a driver who wants to win there has to have the motor and the courage that goes with it. The other tracks are smaller, and the cars go slower, so the wrecks aren't as catastrophic. Thompson's corners are banked at 25 degrees, high enough that winged Midgets barely slow down.

New Jersey was the first state to focus on track safety, and Connecticut was the second. At one time, Thompson was under the jurisdiction of the Connecticut Department of Motor Vehicles, so that meant the track had to use the NASCAR rulebook plus the state's and all its safety rules. "We had to get permitted, licensed for every single event. Every big event, we'd have two inspectors. If there was one light out, there'd be a report, and by next race, they'd have to replace that. Any little thing." The grandstands, fences, and gates had to be certified by an engineer.

In the spring, the track thoroughly inspects every car and puts a sticker on it to show that it meets all the safety requirements. There are two inspectors per division, so each inspection team is specialized.

"Cars are really safe today," says Don, but he acknowledges that accidents happen. "We had the Blewett situation. Total freak accident. They went in kind of deep, and one went into the other. When the car came down through the roof of the other car, it hit him right in the side of the head, through the helmet. Crushed the helmet." Eyewitness accounts of what happened vary, but traumatic brain injury killed John Blewett III because of catastrophic failure of the racecar's safety features.

After Shane Hammond's death, bloggers raised the safety issue at Thompson, that there are no catch fences in the turns or soft walls, that possibly either of those features might have saved Shane's life. "A catch fence would not have helped the Blewetts," says Don. About Shane: "That car went straight in, didn't turn, didn't slide. It went straight into the wall, into the sign we had. No reason to have a catch fence. We have talked about a soft wall but cost and money, cost and money."

There aren't many configurations like Thompson. Most short tracks are more of an oval or circle shape. Thompson is like a paper clip; it has a long straight, a tight turn, another long straight, and another tight turn, each turn exactly balanced.

The biggest expenses of running a track are the purse structure, insurance, property taxes, concessions, electricity, workers' comp, and payroll. The hardest thing about running a track is the weather. Don used to cancel races at the last second, but he changed that policy because teams come from greater distances and have greater expenses. "If you bring them here and send them home, it costs the guy $200 to $300. You have to make the decision earlier in the day. You gotta be careful. It's your reputation." About the drivers, Don says, "If it's cloudy and it may rain and they know they're gonna lose anyway that night, they won't come."

Early cancellations are not just for the teams but for the fans too. "Some people are coming down from New Hampshire, one, one and a half hours, and if they get down here and the gate is closed, it's bad PR."

Back in the day, Don says, he could get 10,000 to 12,000 people to come out for the weekly racing series. "Problem today is it's very difficult to create new race fans. Nobody understands it in short track racing. It's live action entertainment. We created a lot of race fans, and NASCAR has taken them away. They go to the big facilities and see the big stars, and they can't afford to come back here and do both."

Drivers don't think about accidents when they race or about being injured or killed, not if they want to win. Bottom line? Drivers don't have to race. Nobody forces them. NEMA or any other touring organization doesn't have to go to a track it thinks is unsafe; however, drivers love Thompson because, maybe more than anything else, they love going fast, catch fence or no catch fence.

***

"I don't understand that criticism of not having a catch fence there because, basically, there are no grandstands in that area," Mark Arute says about Thompson International Speedway. "In my mind, the fences are there to protect the spectators." Mark is the COO and general manager of Stafford Motor Speedway, the only track in Connecticut with a soft wall—a steel and foam energy reduction system, or SAFER barrier—and only in turn one because, as Mark puts it, the turn is "not user friendly, so to speak. Over the years, we've had some serious incidents. It saves a lot of racecars too."

Mark, 53, is the brother of ESPN and Versus racing reporter Jack Arute Jr. Jack is also the president of the speedway. Mark and Jack have three more brothers and a sister, who are not involved with the track.

The Stafford Springs Agricultural Park opened in 1870 and included a horseracing track. At the end of World War II, it became a dirt track for Midgets and Sprint cars and joined NASCAR in 1959. The owners paved the track in 1967, attracting legendary drivers Ray Hendrick, Richie Evans, Geoff Bodine, Wally Dallenbach, Tim Richmond, Cale Yarbrough, Dale Earnhardt, and Donnie and Bobby Allison.

Mark's father, Jack Sr., was a racecar driver who raced at Thompson, among other tracks in the Northeast. Jack bought the speedway in 1969 and wasted no time making changes that influenced short track racing throughout the country. Against stiff resistance from fans, he started the one tire-one compound rule. To increase car counts and fan interest, he ended the era of late 1930s and 1940s modified jalopies and started the "Pinto Revolution," declaring that fans would rather see Modifieds made out of cars seen on the street. Soon, race teams were running racecars made from chopped down Pintos, Gremlins, and Vegas. After that, Jack invented the SK Modified—the Modified racecar that dominates up and down the East Coast and throughout the South today. Mark became general manager in 1999.

"We take safety very seriously, and we enforce a lot of safety rules that other tracks might not." Mark takes pride in the knowledge and expertise of his safety crew and tech inspectors, John Johnson and Jay Shea—the two Mr. Assholes—and their staff. "We have a group of tech people who are very conscious of parts that are illegal that give one team an advantage over another. We have a considerable amount of diagnostic equipment that enables us to find these infractions. We police fuel. Fuel is a big place where people can spend a lot of money and cheat."

Scott Foster Jr.'s question about why he can't race his Late

Model at all three Connecticut tracks got this response. "It's a good question. We have our rules, which have been the same for many years. One time, the tracks were pretty close on the SK rules, but the other tracks changed things and we didn't, possibly because they don't want to do the tech. They don't want to police the rules."

Mark concedes that it would be feasible if everyone were on the same page tech wise, that it would be possible to standardize the specs for all the different divisions at all the tracks, maybe everywhere in the country, as with Midgets. "Definitely, but each track is maintained by different people with different philosophies. There are some that don't want to do any tech and others that are willing to take the time and spend the money. We've got a significant amount of money invested in equipment that a lot of tracks don't have to police the internal workings of an engine."

Mark went to Ithaca College in Ithaca, New York, and majored in business administration. He has a three-pronged philosophy of running a racetrack:

• Try to satisfy the needs of the competitors. Maintain and create an environment in which they can compete on equal footing, which includes strict enforcement of the rules.

• Take care of the race fans, and give them a good show.

• Keep the racetrack in good shape. "You have to have a facility that your competitors have some pride in to come and participate. With the fans, you have to have some creature comforts."

Mark thinks the key to giving the fans a good show is the speedway's handicapping system for races. "The entertainment value is there because you're not just watching cars go around in a circle. You're watching cars compete and pass. Generally, the faster cars figure out a way to get around the slower cars. The guys with the best equipment and talent find their way to the front, and that's what the excitement is,

I believe, for the race fan."

The handicap formula is straightforward. "There's a dollar value specific to each position the car finishes, so first place gets the most dollars, second place less, and it drops accordingly. You take three weeks worth of racing, and whoever shows the most dollars starts the farthest back. If a competitor misses a week, it's reflected in the dollar amounts, so the system instills loyalty. You want to be here on a regular basis so your handicap won't get hurt. It rewards people that are here. It's a good system."

Mark's father died in 2006, and the family went to court over the racetrack. The brothers and sister not involved in the operation of the track filed a lawsuit against Mark, his wife, Lisa, and brother Jack Jr., claiming they owe them money. Part of the family likes racing, and part doesn't. Do those who don't just want the money?

"Not necessarily. I don't know how you'd categorize it," says Mark. Ah, families. What would we do without families?

Brothers and Other Strangers

"We're building a house," said my mother. "We're moving." We were still living in the two-bedroom house my father built after World War II. My mother and her new husband wanted their own house without the ghost of a previous marriage. I paid little attention to her and Chester Shropshire. He was my stepfather, not my father, and I made sure he knew that. We kept our distance, but that began to change one day when he saved my life.

Chet had settled into our house, and Tim and I started the complicated job of restructuring our family life. Tim, being 7, adapted right away, but I didn't. Chet had usurped my position as man of the house, and I wasn't ready to give it up. To me, Chet looked like a stocky John Wayne. He was 5 feet 8, had served in the Army during World War II, and had been a meat cutter most of his working life. He was my mother's boss at the butcher shop downtown where she had taken a job as a checkout clerk. He had a big laugh and was quiet except when he played cards. He smoked two packs of Kools every day and started each morning with a violent coughing fit and drank four or five Blatz beers a night in front of the TV. He left the discipline to my mother and essentially respected the division between us. Maybe I wasn't the man of the house anymore, but I was the oldest Englehart. That was something. I had to admit that my mother's mood improved after she married Chet. She had a lilting, girlish laugh, and it was good to hear it again.

I was scared to death about entering junior high, and so were my friends, although we never would've admitted it. Merle J. Abbott Elementary School was built in a U shape. The junior high was in the south wing of the school, segregated from the elementary students. In the lower grades, we used to look down the hall, where the middle school kids were, and wonder at the hysteria. Their part of the school even had a different smell, an earthy, musky funk that hung in the air. When we were in fourth grade, the eighth-grade kids looked like grown-ups. By the time we were in sixth grade, they looked downright dangerous.

Dave and I decided that the best way to go into seventh grade was to look tough. We wore our hair long and our collars up, and we smoked Lucky Strikes. We formed a gang called the Savage Saints. I used model airplane paints to paint a red devil—taken from the label on a can of Red Devil lighter fluid—on the backs of matching light blue cotton jackets. We had one other member, Jerry. In pegged pants slung low, pointed-toe shoes, with cigarettes rolled up in our T-shirt sleeves and long greasy hair, we were all show. It was costume. Everything we knew about gangs was from movies, TV, and a couple of older kids in the neighborhood who were true juvenile delinquents—one had spent time in reform school for hijacking a railroad crane—and they were way out of our league. One time we were supposed to rumble with another gang that was either a figment of our imagination or a group of neighborhood 10-year-olds—we weren't sure. Planning our attack provided a few days of excitement. Either way, they didn't show up, which was fine with us.

The eighth graders used two methods to initiate the new seventh graders. One was to smear their faces with lipstick. Girls mostly used it on girls, but a boy could get it too. The other ritual was strictly for boys. A new seventh grader had to shine the eighth grader's shoes, under duress of course. I was in no mood to go through either rite. I looked tough and acted tough.

One day before school started, I was standing in the playground with two friends when an eighth-grade boy came up to me with a bunch of his lackey friends and grabbed me by the neck. He was tall for his age—maybe 6 feet—and had a burr haircut, an ugly scar on his cheek, brown hair, and bad teeth. "Shine my shoes, punk," he said and forced me to the ground at his feet. My friends backed up in terror. The conversation went something like this:

"I said shine my shoes."

I told him politely that he should go have sex with himself. He squeezed my neck harder, pushing my head to the ground. My friends backed away even farther.

"Shine my shoes, asshole."

I repeated my suggestion. He grabbed my arm and bent it behind my back. I wasn't going anywhere until I did what he wanted, so I quietly snorted, cleared my throat, worked up a glob of phlegm from my lungs and mucous from my nose, rolled it into my mouth, and let fly an oyster the size of a golf ball onto his shoe.

Never insult the biggest guy in school in front of his friends. From that day forward, every time he saw me in the hall, he'd slug me, give me the elbow, knock my books out of my hands, anything to let me know he was the alpha dog and felt quite at home picking on someone smaller. I shared no classes with him and went out of my way to avoid him when classes changed. I continued to act tough, but I was scared. This was exactly what I'd been afraid of, being bullied by someone bigger than me, someone I couldn't win over with charm—not that I tried in his case. At the end of the school year, instead of being ecstatic about summer vacation, I dreaded it. The school offered some form of law enforcement. There were people I could go to if things got too bad with Scarface. In the summer, I was on my own. Even worse, Scarface lived three blocks away in a neighborhood on the other side of my school. It would be hard to avoid him.

I had a girlfriend named Jackie, who was a little bit older than me. Pretty, blond, and very shapely in short-shorts. We would meet on the corner by her house because her father hated pubescent boys and didn't want the likes of me to come sniffing around. I wanted to impress this girl with my maturity, and regularly taking a beating in front of her would not work in my favor.

Sacred Heart, the Catholic elementary school in my neighborhood, showed free outdoor movies every Tuesday night in the summer. The school had built a big permanent screen in the field behind the parking lot. Teens and families from blocks around brought homemade popcorn and six-packs of Coke and everyone sat on blankets to watch an old black-and-white Three Stooges short or a color cartoon followed by a comedy or a Western. We weren't there for the flick, although I liked the Three Stooges and the Warner Brothers cartoons. When the sun went down and the movie started, the smooching began. It was all innocent necking; we were surrounded by grown-ups who knew all the kids *and* their parents. After a couple of hours, I'd walk Jackie home and leave her at the corner. She'd tell her father she'd been with her girlfriends.

After the first movie night, I was walking Jackie home, and Scarface came out of nowhere; maybe he'd been stalking me. I ran away like a scared rabbit. I was fast, but he was faster. He caught up with me and slugged me wherever he could. It happened again the following week and again after that. It happened often enough that Jackie broke up with me, certainly embarrassed that her boyfriend was a chicken.

I lived in terror. Finally, I told my mother and Chet what was going on. All they could do was listen. There was no social framework in place for dealing with bullies, and my parents weren't the kind of people who'd call a neighbor and complain about their rotten kid. Chet said I was going to have to fight back. Scarface was bigger, older, taller, and stronger, but I was going to have to stand up to him. He was ruining my life.

I started training in my garage. My grandfather gave me a speed bag that had belonged to Uncle Dick. I hung it from the rafters in the garage and trained every day, punching, working on my timing, quickness, and strength. My hands were small, though. I didn't want to risk breaking my drawing hand with a bad punch, so I concentrated on my footwork. I did kicks and jumps against the garage wall, leaping higher and higher. Maybe I could dodge and weave fast enough to get away from Scarface.

Two friends and I were walking home one night after the movies, and there he was, with his crew. He came loping over to us, but instead of running, I stood my ground in the front yard of a house across the street from the school. He lunged, and I ducked; he grabbed thin air. He was surprised but quickly adapted. He got down low; we circled each other. He lunged again. I moved, spinning out of the way, a karate master without karate. He lunged, I ducked, he missed. Now I was taunting him. I was smiling. I didn't mean to, but I was so proud of myself, I couldn't help it. This went on for several minutes as the humid night air cooled and dew settled on the grass. He swung, my foot slipped, and down I went. He jumped on me, picked me up, and threw me against a tree. It didn't hurt, but I used a time-honored technique that NBA players and professional wrestlers still use today—I faked an injury.

"My back," I cried out in pain, "my back." I pretended to be paralyzed from the waist down.

"I can't feel my legs," I cried, writhing on the wet grass. Scarface and his crew ran away. My friends gathered around me and helped me to my feet. "Are you OK?" asked Dave.

"Yeah, I'm fine." He said he knew I had been faking.

After that, it was back to plan A: running away. There was no stopping Scarface except that he was going to high school in the fall. Maybe that would end the torment. In the meantime, I had to get through the rest of the summer. I was terrified of physical violence, and I'd devoted my life to not being injured. Clearly, I'd taken a wrong turn somewhere.

In the middle of that summer, the school system finished building the new Ben Geyer Junior High and announced that my eighth-grade class, along with the incoming seventh graders, would be moving. We were leaving the school we'd gone to most of our lives to be the first graduating class in some foreign institution south of town. We would have to take a school bus. A school bus? I couldn't think of anything more dweeb-like than riding a school bus. I was too cool to ride.

When the school year started, I walked. It seemed like 20 miles—especially in the winter—but was in fact about a mile and a half away from my home. I could smoke a cigarette and fantasize about girls on the way to school in the morning. I could be on Army patrol slogging through occupied France, driving an expensive sports car, flying my P-40 over Iwo Jima, and thinking up reasons for not doing my homework. I could do a thousand things. School bus. Were they kidding?

None of us liked the new school or the new teachers, and my classmates made sure they knew it. The night of the junior high graduation ceremony, one of the more hated teachers pulled me and a bunch of like-minded hell-raisers aside and told us we would go down in history as the worst class ever to pass through the school. Thank you. It was easy.

Summer again. I hadn't seen Scarface for an entire school year and had forgotten about him. I was about to enter high school and had a new girlfriend. Dances were starting Saturday night in the gym at another neighborhood school, and I was thinking about getting a job and buying a car.

Late one Saturday afternoon, I was walking home from Dave's house. It was hot and sunny, and I was walking with my head down, looking at my very long shadow, and thinking about girls, wondering how I was going to live my life as a freshman in the fall, and fretting over all the things that kept me nervous. I looked up. Scarface blocked the sidewalk. He was alone—no friends he needed to impress, just the two of us. I stopped dead in my tracks. I planned my escape route. He grabbed, I ducked, and the chase was on. I was only a block from home, and I knew I could beat him. I ran as fast as I could down the alley and cut through the Widmer's yard to the sidewalk and into my yard. Scarface was right behind me. I burst through the front door at top speed. And there was Chet, sitting on the couch. "That's him," I yelled, pointing behind me. "That's Scarface."

Chet had taken the day off. He was drinking a beer and watching wrestling on TV. Scarface must've thought I was home alone because when he saw Chet, his eyes opened wide. He stood in the middle of my living room, frozen to the rug. Chet slammed his beer down on the table, put his cigarette in his mouth, got up, grabbed Scarface by the front of his shirt, and, even though Scarface was taller, lifted him high in the air like a side of beef, carried him outside to the front yard, and slammed him to the ground. Scarface was stunned, gasping for breath. I could see the fear in his eyes, and I was enjoying it. Chet grabbed him by the neck, leaned down, and snarled, "If you ever touch him again, I'll kill you."

That was the end of Scarface; I didn't see him again that summer. For the first time, I began to appreciate Chet's presence in my life. I thought maybe this could work out. I was the only kid in the neighborhood with a stepfather, but he could kick ass.

I was more afraid of going to high school than I had been about junior high. High school meant new kids from tough neighborhoods. I looked tough, but let's face it, I was a poseur. I'd never spent time in the slammer, and some of these high school kids had. I decided to clean up my act. I'd go into high school looking like a preppy—or at least my version of one. I got a haircut and asked my mother to buy me some shirts with button-down collars and a pair of conservative penny loafers for school.

The first day at South Side High School, we had short 15-minute periods to become acclimated to the much bigger school. When I walked into gym class, I almost had a heart attack. There was Scarface. Oh, God, no, I thought, not gym class, any class but gym. When he saw me, he came right up to me, stuck out his hand, and said, "Welcome to South Side." He was smiling. "If anybody gives you a hard time, let me know, and I'll take care of him." From bully to protector. I didn't know if Chet had put the fear of God into him or if he'd found religion on his own or liked my new style or what, but I never had any trouble with him again.

***

I didn't care about leaving the old neighborhood—I'd be

glad to get out—but the thought of leaving the house I had grown up in, the room where I'd conquered death, was depressing. The idea of leaving my high school was even worse. I was near the end of my first year. I had made more friends and was starting to get a lot of attention for my artistic ability. We would be moving to a different school district, and I'd have to go to Elmhurst High School, where the students were a bunch of farmers and hicks. My mother and father and an uncle had gone to South Side. My history teacher and gym teacher had taught them. My aunt, who worked for the school board, pulled a few strings, and I was allowed to stay at my old school, but I had to find my own transportation, which meant bumming a ride every day from Chet and my mother when they drove to work. I couldn't wait until I got my driver's license.

We moved into a suburban, three-bedroom, ranch-style house in Siberia. The new subdivision outside town was called Lakeshores, although there were no shores because there was no lake. None of the neighborhood kids were my age, just a bunch Tim's age and younger. I had mixed feelings about the new house. It had no basement, but it was bigger than our old house, and Tim and I finally had our own bedrooms. The move did one thing, though; it brought Tim and me closer.

I was 5 when Tim was born. I don't remember much about it except for the night it happened. My mother ran naked from her bedroom, her big belly bouncing, and a towel between her legs, yelling, "My water broke. My water broke." Water? What water? Talk about confused feelings. I was afraid and curious at the same time. Until then, I'd never seen either of my parents naked.

What happened next is foggy. I think my grandparents came over to watch me that night. The next thing I remember is looking at Tim, fresh from the hospital in his bassinette, a crying, squirmy little pink loaf. I think I gave him about 60 seconds and then went back to drawing pictures.

Although our age difference didn't allow for any mutual friends, we played together in the house. When he was old enough, we had fake fights and racecar adventures and did pretty much all the things that brothers do. Sometimes, we had real fights.

Baby-sitting Tim was always easy money because he played outside most of the time, and I could hang around the house, watch TV, and draw pictures. One day not long after we moved into our new house, I was in a foul adolescent mood. I had just finished washing and waxing the dining room floor, something my mother had ordered me to do if I wanted to be paid for the day. It was Saturday morning, and I was stuck until Chet and my mother got home from work in the late afternoon. I was sitting at the dining room table reading the comics page when Tim came through the door from the garage with mud on his shoes.

"Hey," I said. "I just waxed this floor. Don't walk on it."

"What?" he said, walking toward me.

"I said I just waxed the floor. Stop."

"What?" he said again, still walking. He was giving me that vacant, challenging, stop-me-if-you-can look. He was 9 and going through an intense asshole period. I knew what he was doing. I'd been there.

I jumped up from the table, grabbed him by the shirt, and pushed him toward the door. He called me a name. I don't remember now what it was—probably one I taught him. I picked him up, carried him into the bathroom, stuck his head in the toilet, and flushed. It started a family tradition that would come up again.

In the summer between my junior and senior years of high school, my mother dropped a bomb. She was pregnant. A half sibling was on the way. Sure, why not? Tim and I were astonished that our mother, the woman we'd known all our lives, was going to have a baby. That conjured up visions of her and Chet actually having sex, which was not something I wanted stuck in my brain. It made me want to move out of the house even sooner.

With the help and guidance of my art teacher, Mrs. Fleck, I'd been working toward a scholarship to the American Academy of Art in Chicago, but scholarship or not, I was determined to go to art school somewhere, even if I had to pay my own way to the Fort Wayne Art School. Now, with the stork on the way, I upped the ante and decided that I would move out of the house when I graduated and get an apartment whether I went to art school or not. Near the end of the first semester, the advertising agency that sponsored the scholarship—after checking with Mrs. Fleck to make sure I wasn't a professional artist—announced that I had won.

I was 18 when Ritchie was born, a graduating senior, certain I knew everything there was to know about life and love. I had one foot out the door, had won a full one-year scholarship to the American Academy of Art, and was engaged to my high school sweetheart, Judy King, the only child of a mother who'd been married four times—twice to the same man—and who had a father in Illinois with his second wife.

I barely noticed the new kid, this half brother added to the mix of step this and step that, half sister, half brother, half-crazy family. By the time I was a junior in high school, I'd sworn off my juvenile-delinquent ways; as a senior, I went back to the collegiate style I wore as a freshman: cardigan sweater, medium-length hair, loafers, and white button-down collar shirt. I had always been a serious student in the subjects I liked—art, history, social studies, science, and business—and miserable in English and math. That last year, I buckled down with the other subjects as well, earning all A's and B's on my report card for the first time since elementary school.

After high school, I saw my new little brother Ritchie on weekend visits home from art school, but mostly he was a curiosity item, like a new puppy, only in diapers. Chet and I grew closer as he and my mother delighted in the new baby. I had matured enough to see a different side of Chet, the father of a small child, the big man made tender, vulnerable. I saw the future stretch out before me, a golden road to riches and family happiness.

Temporary Sanity

My grandfather never called, ever, not when I was living two miles away in Fort Wayne and certainly not now that I was living in Chicago, going to art school, settling in to married life. At first, I thought something had happened to my mother. "Chet died," my grandfather said.

Chet had been at work when he started having chest pains. He was managing the meat department in a new supermarket, and my mother worked for him. She was there when he nearly collapsed. The owner of the supermarket called an ambulance right away, and Chet was awake and talking when the attendants wheeled him into the emergency room, but when the doctor gave him a shot, his eyes rolled back and his heart stopped. The staff tried frantically to resuscitate him.

Chet was 39 years old. He liked to smoke and drink and was probably 25 pounds overweight, but an autopsy revealed that his heart arteries were too small, a birth defect he lived with all his life and didn't know he had.

My family spent the funeral in a daze. Chet was so

young—his hair was still dark—and he'd died so suddenly that the funeral home put very little makeup on him. In the coffin, he looked as he had when he fell asleep on the couch watching TV. I expected him to wake up and trudge off to bed.

I was in the first semester of my second year but told my mother I'd quit and move back home to care for her. "You most certainly will not," she said, angry that I'd even suggested it. I was in the process of borrowing money for the second semester, and my mother was planning to co-sign a loan for me. The future was suddenly up in the air. My mother—a widow at 41—had a toddler to raise, and I wanted to do *something*. After all, once I had been the man of the house. I could do it again.

After Chet's funeral, I returned to Chicago with my young wife. My mother, cast again into the single-parent life, didn't wait long before she started dating. I remember one guy with dark hair whose name is lost to time, but for the most part, I didn't know whom she was seeing. During that time, my mother, Ritchie, and Tim began going to the church that the Engleharts went to, reestablishing my mother's ties with my father's family. They had always been fond of her.

One weekend, she brought Ritchie, Tim, and Charles Bowers—Chuck—to visit my wife and me in Chicago and to announce that she and Chuck were getting married. He seemed like a nice enough guy, had a friendly smile, and was reasonably handsome. Chuck had made his career as a salesman in the graphic arts industry working for a commercial engraving company in Fort Wayne, so we had something to talk about. Like my mother, he'd been married twice before, although both marriages had ended in divorce.

He had three grown children, a son and a daughter who lived in Fort Wayne and a son who lived in Colorado.

Chuck seemed to enjoy the role of being father to a toddler, and Ritchie called him dad.

Ritchie and I grew closer when my son, Mark Allen—his middle name is the same as Tim's—was born a year later. Three years after that, my daughter, Sherri Lynn, who was named after a stepsister and my half sister, was born. Ritchie was unique in my family—a 3-year-old uncle—but in Indiana at that time, folks got married young. Uncles who were younger than their nieces and nephews weren't unusual.

I envied Ritchie slightly—or maybe it was a case of latent sibling rivalry. I saw a progression from me, the oldest, the biggest pain in the ass to my mother, to Tim, who got more from my parents than I had, to Ritchie, the baby, who got everything he wanted. The only thing Ritchie would eat was spaghetti, so my mother would cook a dinner for the family and a special spaghetti dinner for him. He got a BB gun when he was maybe 11 or 12, and then he got two gas-powered air rifles when he was a little older.

When I was 12, I tried for weeks to talk my parents into buying me a BB gun, but my mother wouldn't hear of it. It didn't help my argument when Dave came over with his BB gun while I was baby-sitting Tim, and we shot out the basement windows. OK, bad judgment. Maybe she was right, but Ritchie got more than Tim and I had. He had a phone in his room, for chrissake, and a race-ready kart in the garage. At his age, I would've killed for a kart.

My only recourse was to tease the hell out of him. He went through a phase when he didn't like certain smells: paint thinner, certain kinds of glue, vinegar, spray paint, garlic. Foul odors of any kind would send him running out of the room in a wrinkled-nose fit. My favorite thing to do was to grab his forearm, lick it, and then tell him to smell it. I don't know what it is—maybe the combination of mouth bacteria and skin bacteria—but it smells to high heaven, worse than shit.

After Tim graduated from high school, he put in a brief stint as an apprentice union glazer. When he was laid off for the second time, he and his cat, which liked to pee on my dining room rug, moved in with my wife and me in the Chicago suburb of Arlington Heights. Tim hadn't lived there too long before he started dating Peg, the girl he'd marry. I worked at the *Chicago American*, the former *Herald American*—Ben Hecht and Charles MacArthur's inspiration for *The Front Page*—which later changed its name to *Chicago Today*. When I had built enough freelance business to start a studio, I sold the Arlington Heights house and moved my family back to Fort Wayne. Chuck found office space for my business and a couple of accounts drawing labels for egg cartons for a distributor and illustrations of funeral parlors for condolence cards and the covers of their programs. I opened my art studio and drew editorial cartoons for the *Journal-Gazette* on the side, hired my father to keep my books, bought a new house in the suburbs, and leased a hot Chevy Camaro. I gloried in the thrill of reaching my adolescent goal of having my own commercial art studio, a new house in the suburbs, and a young family at the age of 27.

It all seemed normal now—even with all the steps and halves—a nuclear family nearby, holidays spent across town with relatives, not hundreds of miles away with friends, although holidays and birthdays were crazy. Between blood relatives and steps, the schedule was full. Chet's family became former steps. I drifted away from them but still had a mob of relatives, new step relatives, and in-laws. The family joke was that my children called any woman over 40 grandma.

I drew a Thanksgiving Day cartoon based on my experience for the *Hartford Courant*. It's a picture of a family leaving the front door of the house and heading toward the car in the driveway, four kids leading the way. The wife is holding a pie, and the husband is reading a printout that says, "First we go to your mother and stepfather's house. Then we go to my father and stepmother's. Then we go to your father and stepmother's and then to my mother and stepfather's. Your ex will pick up your kids there and bring them home tonight. On the way home, we leave my kids with my ex and pick them up tomorrow. I worked it out on the computer."

When Ritchie was around 10 years old, he went into a predictable asshole period, just as Tim and I had. He had the same pineapple haircut and skinny body we'd had at that age. One day when Ritchie was being particularly obnoxious, Tim looked at me and said, "Toilet?" We grabbed Ritchie, dragged him into the bathroom, stuck his head in the toilet, and flushed. When Ritchie looks back on it now, he laughs when he tells the story. "Actually, it was kind of interesting," he says. "I'd never seen under the rim of the toilet before."

I took him to see a USAC Midget race at Baer Field Speedway in Fort Wayne, his first visit to a racetrack. The track had been built the year he was born, and I'd been to it only once. South Anthony had been torn down to make way for an apartment complex, Fort Wayne Speedway had closed years earlier, and Baer Field was the only track left in town. It sat next to the municipal airport, Baer Field, named after a pioneering Hoosier pilot who flew with the Lafayette Escadrille in World War I.

I don't remember anything about the race other than that Ritchie loved it. After that, we went maybe once or twice a year until I decided to switch careers and become a full-time editorial cartoonist. I had reached my goal; I had my art studio and three full-time employees. I was making good money as a commercial artist and cartoonist, but freelancing editorial cartoons for the *Journal-Gazette* was infinitely more rewarding than everything else. A recession hit the country in 1974, and when it got to Fort Wayne, I lost some key accounts and had to lay off my staff. I thought it was a good time to switch careers. I approached the paper about a full-time gig, but it couldn't afford to pay me enough to support a family of four in the style to which we'd all become accustomed, so I contacted editorial cartoonist friends and found a job in Dayton, Ohio, at the *Journal-Herald*. Soon, we were back to traveling for weekend visits and holidays.

As complicated as it was, my family had stabilized. Again, it didn't last long. Shortly after the move to Dayton, my mother learned she had breast cancer. A high-strung woman, she had never been a smoker or drinker, but she'd never been in perfect health either—appendix out, gall bladder too. When I was very young, she had what the family called a nervous breakdown, but she'd never had a life-threatening disease until now. This was not in the plan I had mapped out for my future. I'd willed my success through working hard, reaching goals, and stumbling into good luck. My mother had been through enough, what with divorce and widowhood; she would live to a ripe old age in a stable and secure family.

Surgeons removed her breast and assured the family that they had gotten the entire tumor. A couple of years later, they removed the other breast. Then, not long after that, doctors told her that the cancer had spread to her colon, that it was scattered throughout her intestines and inoperable. She had two years to live.

When Chuck told me the bad news, I fell into the same bottomless pit that claimed me when I saw Shane Hammond wreck. How could God do this to her, to my family, to me? What would happen to Ritchie, his father gone and now his mother? I asked my mother what to do about him. She said, "Don't worry. He's not your responsibility."

Her father—my grandfather—had died several years ear-lier. He and my grandmother had been married for 60-some years but not without controversy. In keeping with the family tradition, my grandfather was Protestant and divorced when they married. My grandmother was Catholic and so excommunicated for the sin of marrying a divorced man. She was still alive when my mother was diagnosed. She helped my mother as much as she could, but her mobility was limited. She didn't talk much. She laughed at most of my jokes, but we all could see that my mother's health crisis weighed on her. No parent wants to see a child die first. That's not how it's supposed to work. Then, as we all prepared for a tragic future, my mother called. "Grandma died."

My mother had not heard from Grandma that day, so she and Chuck went to her house. They found her at the bottom of the attic stairs. At first, they thought she'd fallen down the stairs, but an autopsy revealed that she'd had a heart attack and then fell. The casket was closed when the family came to view her the day before the wake. A framed formal photo of her sat on top of the casket, but it wasn't enough. The funeral director said she had a disfiguring injury on the side of her face. We grandchildren wanted the casket open, so the funeral director promised to do some work on her that night. Before the start of viewing the following day, we viewed her. I didn't know what the practitioners of the fune-real arts had done, but she looked fine, like Grandma. The casket stayed open.

I beat a path back and forth from Dayton to Fort Wayne to see my mother as much as I could; we didn't have a lot of time left together. One night in Fort Wayne, after everyone had gone to bed, my mother and I were talking, and I broke down. All the years of fighting with her, defying her, being angry with her for divorcing my father just drained out of me into tears. She said, "I know it's hard on those left behind." She had made peace with her fate, but I hadn't.

Over time, we had cleared the air between us. When my high school sweetheart and I made plans to marry—she was 18, I was 19—my father wrote a three-page letter trying to talk me out of it. We were too young, give it some time, think of your future, she's not pregnant is she? I was still furious with my parents for divorcing. I was going to show them how to put together a marriage that worked. I wrote a terse note to my father saying don't worry, you won't have to pay for the wedding. Now, late at night, 16 years later, my mother told me she had asked him to write that letter. She had never said a word to me before. My mother had been a young bride, and I knew she loved my wife like a daughter, but I'd had no idea she was against my marriage. I'd assumed she approved, not that it would've changed anything if she hadn't. I was going to carry on the family tradition, except for the divorce. I was better than that.

Then my mother dropped another bombshell. She had been abused as a child. My grandfather had beaten her with his belt for the flimsiest reasons. Her brother, Uncle Del, ruefully confirmed it a few years later. "Dad would just whale on her," he said.

Another thing—her family never celebrated birthdays, not hers, neither of her parents', or her brothers'. I thought back and couldn't remember our celebrating hers or my father's. She'd always made a big deal out of Tim's, Ritchie's, and mine, but her birthday was a mystery.

I'd had no idea about any of this. Nobody had said anything, ever. I had a close relationship with my mother's parents, visited often, mowed their lawn for cash, and borrowed money to buy tires for my car. They taught me how to still fish with a bamboo pole and how to put a worm on the hook when I was little. My grandfather was a hero to me; he'd saved the life of a co-worker in the railroad yards when a boxcar accidentally rolled over the man's leg, severing it. Grandpa took off his bootlace and made a tourniquet to stop the bleeding. It was reported in both newspapers.

The grandparents I loved—revered even—were child abusers. This explained my mother's nervous demeanor, her inability to relax, her inability to discipline me and make it stick. Maybe it even explained why she and my father got divorced. I had figured her personality came from all the coffee she drank. Her standard phrase was, "You just don't realize." She was right. I didn't.

She was 56 when she died. Ritchie was 16. She died in June, a week before my son's 13th birthday. My father came to her funeral and sat in the front row with us. I'd never seen him cry before. In the fall, my wife and kids and I, Tim and his family, and Chuck and Ritchie tried to have Thanksgiving together, but it was a disaster. The loss of my mother left a void we couldn't fill. Some families have a member who's the glue, the linchpin, the person who holds it all together. That's what my mother was to me, to all of us. When she died, the whole structure collapsed. I began to feel that my family had died with her.

What had started simply as my mother, father, Tim, and me along with uncles, aunts, cousins, and grandparents became all that plus a teeming array of steps and halves. After Chet died, my new stepfather, Chuck, joined the family with his three kids, whom I barely knew. It was too much. After my mother died, he raised Ritchie as his own son until Ritch grew up and moved away. Eventually, Chuck remarried, and we lost contact.

Ritchie and I exchanged Christmas cards but didn't see each other much after my mother died; I rarely went back to Fort Wayne. Then my father and his second wife divorced. In time, he married a woman who'd been married before and had two kids, both adopted. I've tried to do a flow chart of all this, but I get a severe case of writer's cramp and a headache.

In 1980, my wife and I moved our family to Connecticut, and four years later, we split up, fracturing the family even further. After a couple of years of bachelorhood, I married Pat McGrath, who has one son, four brothers, and a large number of relatives, adding about three dozen more members to the family unit. I took Pat to Fort Wayne to introduce her to my extensive family, blood, step, half, and otherwise, but the distance has pretty much kept us away from Indiana since. Over the years, I called Ritchie every Christmas just to stay in touch and listen to him complain about his job and politics. I always invited him to come visit us in Connecticut because I knew he'd love the state-of-the-art racing here, but the East Coast was outside his comfort zone. He'd drive to Indy and to Michigan International Speedway for a NASCAR event, but Connecticut was too far, too foreign.

One year, it dawned on me that he never called; I was always the one who made the call. I decided not to call just to see how long it would take him to call me. I know I was being childish; brothers can be that way. Tim and I stayed in touch, and he stayed in touch with Ritchie. Tim and I got together in Indiana to play golf with our father once a year and occasionally have an Englehart family reunion. I decided that because Ritchie never came to visit me in Connecticut, I wasn't going to make the effort to see him in Fort Wayne. When I told Tim about seeing Shane Hammond's wreck and how it had affected me, he told me Ritchie was working on a Modified crew at Baer Field Speedway. I gave in and called. It had been ten years since we had talked on the phone, 15 since we'd talked face to face.

Baer Field

It's mid-August, a typically hot, humid summer evening in Indiana on a day that seems to get warmer as the sun goes down. The cornfields that line the road to Baer Field Speedway thrum with a high-pitched chorus of insects, but as I get closer, the roar of racecars easily drowns them out. Ritchie has worked on Ron Stine's Modified crew for four years. In typical short track fashion, Ritchie, Ron's dad, Ron's brother, Ron's daughter, her boyfriend, and Ron's girlfriend make up the team. Ron, always a force in any race, in any kind of racecar, owns the track speed record for Modifieds and was the 2007 champion in the division.

Baer Field, an airport that in my day looked like a bus station, had gone semi big time since I'd last flown there, remodeling and expanding, changing its name to Fort Wayne International Airport because it had a flight to Toronto. The main runway is hard up against the parking lot of the racetrack, which is right next door on the other side of the wire fence.

The large sign at the track entrance says, "Welcome to

Baer Field Speedway. No refunds." This is my idea of an out-law track. Not sanctioned by NASCAR—or any organization in its right mind—it's as fast as any half-mile track in New England. Other than deteriorating considerably, the place hasn't changed much since Dick Trickle, Dale Jarrett, Mark Martin, Dale Earnhardt, and Eddie Doyle raced there back in the day. Fans sit on worn wooden bleachers and look through a rusty catch fence along the front straight, which is only a few feet from the first row. There are still no catch fences in the turns, no guardrails, no walls, no anything, just the dark night when a driver goes too wide and slips over the edge. A driver who goes far enough in turn one ends up in the woods and will be lucky not to hit a tree, which one Modified famously did. Turns two, three, and four are in a cornfield. The track is a half-mile, semi-banked oval with a 3/8-mile track in the infield for the beginner divisions and a kart track inside that. A motocross track winds around the perimeter of the parking lot.

Ritch meets me at the pit gate. He still looks like that spaghetti-eating little kid, except he's in his mid-40s and thick around the middle. He wears a mustache and still has a full head of dark brown hair. He shows me around the weathered grandstands and points out the crumbling concrete wall that holds the catch fence on the front straight. The place looks as though it hasn't been maintained, painted, or upgraded since it was built. Everything made of wood has faded to the color of dry rot. Old telephone poles hold up the rickety, double-decked array of wooden sponsors' signs in the infield. The contraption looks as if it would fall over in the wake of a passing racecar. Light poles lean left and right; at first glance, not one of them looks vertical. White-painted, concrete-block buildings house the bathrooms and the concession stand. The sign over the door of a large metal building says "Beer Barn."

Ron's out on the track, driving hot laps in his red-and-yellow number 3 with four other cars. I examine the litter-strewn walkways and the broken retaining-wall supports where the catch fence is attached, thinking that the front row in the bleachers here is the last place I'd want to sit, unless I wanted to catch a flying Late Model or Modified in my lap. Being in a racecar would be safer; at least there's some protection. I hear Ritchie groan. I look to the track and don't see anything amiss. What happened? "Ron got pinched into the wall," Ritchie says. I look to the track again and see the culprit, a Modified with "Asphalt Angel" hand painted on the back.

Ron leaves the track and drives into the paddock. "He's going to be pissed," says Ritch. When Ron is pissed, the crew leaves him alone. His girlfriend can talk him down, but everyone else gives him space. Molly Ketzler, tall and attractive, is much younger than Ron and wears sparkles on her eyelids and a "Ron Stine 3" T-shirt. She knows just what to say and, more important, what *not* to say. Back in Eddie Doyle's day, girls weren't allowed in the pits. They, along with green-colored racecars, cash money, and peanuts, were considered bad luck.

Ritchie rides shotgun and directs me as I drive my rental car, a Chevy HHR that I call the Health and Human Resources—who names these cars anyway?—to the paddock. The paddock at Baer Field Speedway is behind the back straight. Because of the way the track is laid out, once people are in the paddock, they're there for the night. When the racing starts, the access road from the front-straight bleachers is closed; there's no connection to the main grandstands, toilets, or snack bar. A small trailer in the paddock sells over-cooked hamburgers, drinks, and potato chips. There are no men's and women's bathrooms, but plenty of beat-up old urine-soaked Porta-Johns are available. God help the crewmember, driver, or fan who has to go number two in one of those things.

The paddock is mostly gravel, and brown weeds grow between the broken concrete slabs used for parking race-cars. The old asphalt-paved lane to the track entrance on the backstretch is crazed and cracked like desert hardpan. At Connecticut tracks, a Sunoco tanker the size of a septic service truck sits in the pits, selling 113-octane racing fuel at $9 a gallon. An additional tanker filled with methanol shows up when the Midgets and Supermods come to town. Baer Field Speedway has a fuel dump; 55-gallon drums are stacked in and around an open box trailer that has a gas pump, a Sunoco flag on one side, and an American flag on the other, waving in the breeze. The gas is $6 a gallon.

When Ron was a kid, his father built him a go-kart out of an old ironing board and a Briggs & Stratton lawnmower motor. Ron's love of driving fast was born. His mother and father took him to races at Anderson Speedway and Avilla Speedway. They were spectators, but Ron wanted to drive. A friend of his was racing at a dirt track in a 1969 Pontiac Bonneville two-door with stock tires and a roll cage added for safety. Ron bought it and went to school on that car. They raced at Baer Field in a class called Detroit Iron. He did well enough but got a little crazy and wrecked the car in the last race of the season when he tangled with a lapped car. Another friend had a '72 Chevelle Street Stock racing at Avilla. The friend wrecked and broke his wrist, but he had sponsors and asked Ron to take the wheel for the rest of the season. Ron finished third in his first race. His friend "was kind of bummed that we did so much better than he did with it," says Ron. Eventually, his friend wanted out of racing, so Ron traded a small-block Chevy racing motor for the car and started his career in the seat. In 1991, he won the division in Hobby Stocks. "It was a good, fun class."

After that, Ron decided to race in the Late Model division at Baer Field with a different car, an '88 Monte Carlo body on a race chassis. He won the most features, the most-

Ron Stine sits in his car cooling off after being pinched into the wall during hot laps at Baer Field Speedway. (Photo by the author)

popular-driver award, and the championship in his division. Then he dropped out of racing to start his own business, an auto repair shop that lasted for eight years before he closed it. The Monte Carlo sat in his garage until Baer Field held an open race one Saturday night. Ron dusted off the car, which had been on jack stands for almost a decade, and led most of the race. "I couldn't believe how good we ran against them, so that kind of set the hook again."

He bought a used Modified in 2004 and rebuilt it through the winter. "The reason I went that route is because you can run them just about anywhere. Throughout this part of the country, everybody's got them at every track. Kind of an open-motor rule that I like. I didn't like the two-barrel stuff." In 2006, he won rookie of the year and driver of the year and was third in points.

This season, Ron is going through a bitter divorce. His future ex-wife kicked him out of the house with nothing but five days' worth of clothes, his toothbrush, a coffeepot, and, most important, his Modified.

Ron describes himself as an old-school driver. "I'm aggressive to a certain point. I'm not going to purposely wreck somebody unless they piss me off. Use the bumper when you have to. I'm a little conservative when it comes to running over people to gain a position." What goes around comes around, though, and if he has to, he'll play payback. Ron says he's not superstitious, "but I do catch myself talking about luck a lot."

Ron likes Mark Martin as a role model in NASCAR. "He's a good driver. He's aggressive, but he won't go out of his way to wreck somebody. I kind of like old-school things, and he's part of the old-school realm now. I don't like change in a lot of ways. I wish NASCAR was like it used to be. I was an Earnhardt fan back when. I liked his driving style. He was aggressive and wasn't afraid to show it. I'm not real keen on some of these young guys that are in there. They got cocky attitudes and everything. They walk around like they have a chip on their shoulder. I don't follow it like I used to."

Ron needs to put money into his racecar. The motor needs refreshing, the carburetor needs rebuilding, and the car needs tires, but he's strapped for cash. Divorce isn't cheap. He talks about maybe quitting, maybe taking a season off. His job at the GM truck plant is in jeopardy because of layoffs and the bad economy.

The Great Recession is just beginning and already has affected car counts at Baer Field. Only 14 Modifieds will line up for the feature tonight. Ritchie is preoccupied, measuring tire temperatures, jacking up the car, bending, prying metal, straightening what he can, and trying to fix the damage that Asphalt Angel had done earlier.

At this time of year, the sun sets directly behind the Baer Field grandstands. At a certain point before the sun dips below the horizon, the grandstands and the fans are silhouetted against the great orange globe. It would make a dramatic photo with the right camera, but it's almost impossible to watch the cars on the track from the pits—even sunglasses don't help. The Indiana Air National Guard is on maneuvers today, and the screaming F-16 Falcons make the racecars seem slow and puny. As the planes rocket down the runway, those Pratt & Whitney F100-PW-200 engines drown out the sound of the racecars. The roar of jets taking off, the angry snarl of racecars, the smells of auto exhaust, jet exhaust, and burned rubber, the intense light of the sun in my eyes—it's the front porch to heaven.

I look to the infield and ask myself, "What's wrong with this picture?" There's a wrecker, certainly, and a couple of pickups but no ambulance. In Connecticut, it's customary—or maybe it's the law—to have at least two ambulances ready to take injured drivers to the nearest hospital, and many have made the trip. At Baer Field there's a fire department rescue squad in the darkness behind turn two but no ambulances. I ask Ritch about it. "There's a fire station less than a mile away. They got an ambulance."

The rules for the Modifieds at Baer Field are few. There are some weight requirements, but there are no radios, no mirrors, no limits on tires, and no limits on motors. "You can put any big motor you want in there, but it's just going to light up the tires," says Ritch. Ron runs a 355-cubic-inch Chevy with a Holley four-barrel. He works second shift—

"second trick" they call it in Fort Wayne—at the truck plant and has custody of his teenage daughter. Between working, racing, and single parenthood, he's spread pretty thin.

Even with his limited budget, Ron is a competitive driver in the Modified division. Tonight, in spite of the hot lap incident, he qualifies fourth in the time trials with a time of 18.642, or 96.555 mph. I don't know why tracks insist on giving results in time rather than miles per hour. Miles per hour is easier to relate to. What does 18 or 19 seconds mean? It takes me 15 minutes to drive to the grocery store. Speed, however, is another matter. I've driven at 96.555 miles per hour. Many people have. Not on an oval track in the heat of competition but on the highway in my own car. Miles per hour says so much more than time. It makes people like me think they can be racecar drivers.

The Street Stocks run their first heat race, but on the second lap, two cars tangle in turn four, hopelessly locking bumpers. The wreckers are quick on the scene, but it takes 40 minutes to free the racecars. Ritchie was so young when Chet died that he doesn't remember him, so he loves to hear stories about his dad. While we're waiting for the safety crew to clean up the wreck, I tell Ritchie of how I began to appreciate his father as my stepfather when he saved my ass from the big bully, Scarface.

The cars in the Baer Field paddock start their motors for the first Modified heat race. Ron climbs through the window, buckles his five-point harness, and settles into his racecar. Molly gives him a kiss through the driver's window before he puts on his helmet and she hooks the net. This is their ritual before every race.

Ron's race doesn't turn out well. After a few laps, he pulls off the track into the paddock. The car isn't right, and when the crew members put it up on jack stands and crawl underneath, they can see the frame is slightly bent near the gas tank from the hot laps pinch against the wall. They can't bend the frame in the pits. They'll have to set up the car to compensate.

Ritchie has an affinity for racing tires. "I'm really good at setting up the tires when it's 90 degrees or hotter," he says. It was at least that on this evening, and a haze of exhaust and humidity hung over the track all night. The crew works its magic, and Ron comes in third in the feature, finishing the weekend third in points for the season.

When the last race ends, pit road is opened from the grandstands. Friends and family pour in, some walking, some driving pickups, and some driving passenger cars. Tim and his wife, Peg, join us in the paddock. We can't remember the last time the brothers have all been together, maybe that final Thanksgiving so long ago. After our mother died and Chuck was raising him, Ritchie naturally gravitated toward Chuck's family, but Ritchie still had Shropshire aunts and uncles living nearby, as well as a few cousins. After our mother died, he went to the races at Bear Field and Avilla with his half sisters, who were old enough to buy alcohol. They mixed batches of sloe screws—sloe gin and orange juice—smoked pot, and stayed at the tracks partying until three in the morning.

Seeing Ritchie reminds me of my mother and the brief time we all had together as an extended family, the Thanksgivings, Christmases, Easters, the birthdays. After she died and before I moved east, I went to the Republican National Convention in Detroit and the Democratic National Convention in New York City and started a job search. I stayed busy. When the job at the *Courant* came along, the fit was perfect, and I couldn't turn it down. Maybe I was fleeing rather than coping, but I left the Midwest in a hurry.

Ritchie, Tim, and I had lost our mother, and we couldn't do anything about it. Ritchie had lost his father as a toddler and his mother as a teenager. So much loss in one family. I wondered about losing a brother in a freak accident, an accident I witnessed, or worse, an accident I was a part of. What would that be like? What would I do about *that?*

Helpless

His handshake is filled with rage. It's firm, no nonsense, and hurried. Jimmy Blewett likes to keep moving, going here, going there, visiting friends in the paddock, heading to the autograph table, striding down the midway with another driver. He pauses for only a second. He wears a black fire suit and a black cap turned backward. Black sunglasses hide his blue eyes. He's tall and muscular and has a boyish face, a thick neck, and broad shoulders. When he's not in motion, he lifts weights in his hauler between races. Pumping iron, driving iron, recycling iron—he and his brother, John III, co-owned the family scrap metal business where they worked in Howell, New Jersey. Grandfather John Blewett, a driver, taught his son John Blewett Jr. to drive who taught his son John III who taught his younger brother, Jimmy. A company that sells Peterbilt and Mack trucks sponsors him. His hauler is the nicest in the paddock, a big red-and-white one with his orange number 12 decaled on the side. It typically carries two racecars, a Whelen Tour Modified and an SK Modified. It's been less than a year—11 months to be

exact—since the Blewett brothers wrecked in turn one at
Thompson.

This night at Stafford Motor Speedway, in the 50-lap
SK feature race, Jimmy starts near the back and battles to
mid-pack and then to fourth but gets into the rear of a car
in turn one. Wheels touch, and he goes flying. Everyone in
the stands holds their collective breath, thinking of the fatal
wreck with his brother last year. This time, no damage, no
caution flag, but a wreck on the backstretch stops the race.
After 15 minutes of cleanup, the race restarts and the green
flag drops. Jimmy's racecar is different, slower and looser
than it was before the wreck. He fades with every lap, finishing out of the top ten. After the race, he drives off the track
to his pit area, and I follow. When he shuts off his car and
squirms out the driver's window, I ask him what happened
to his car.

"Piece of shit," he yells, his red face making his blue eyes
glare. "Fucking $60,000 racecar piece of shit. You can put
that in your newspaper." Ah, I wish I could. It's one of the
most honest post-race comments I've ever heard.

"Men have a harder time with sadness," says Helen Balaban. She's not a racecar driver; she's a licensed professional
counselor. Over her career, she's counseled everyone from
children to the families of 9/11 victims. Helen flies all over
the country as part of an employee assistance program. If
a worker commits suicide on the job or an armed robber
knocks off a bank and the staff is traumatized, in comes
Helen. I told her about my reaction to seeing Shane Hammond's accident and how I felt later, about the vague, free-
floating anger I couldn't shake.

"Women will cry freely and talk to a girlfriend. For men,
it's more macho to go it alone. Men will cry, just not in
public. Men mask sadness with anger. It's easier that way."
Maybe not easier but more satisfying; for years, Pat's Toyota

carried a dent in the dashboard where I had hit it with my fist. Helen explains my reaction to seeing a traumatic event, such as Shane Hammond's wreck. "The initial response of disbelief: you see it, your mind is telling you and showing you what's there. You see this young man flying through the air in what seemed to be a very tragic way that he died. This was very dramatic, and you were in shock and disbelief. Most people would say it feels like you're in the *Twilight Zone*. It's like you're there, but you're not there, like a dream state."

Helen says the fact that I felt physically sick usually comes later to accompany grief. What I felt was a reaction to seeing a traumatic event, but I'm like that. When I see someone injured or bandaged or with a fresh scar, I feel it in my testicles. Maybe I'm just physically empathetic. I don't know. Watching *America's Funniest Home Videos* is mildly painful.

"Once the shock wears off, some people start to feel chest pains," says Helen. "As long as the pain doesn't radiate, it's usually the body's way of relating to trauma." Others will have upper- or lower-back pain, joint pain, knee pain, pain in the wrists and sometimes fingers. Migraine headaches are common after people witness trauma. Each person's body reacts in different ways. "Usually, the place where your body is weakest, that's where emotions will attack." My stomach and my balls are my weakest parts? That's not reassuring.

"We also feel the impact behaviorally—sleep disorders, restlessness, inability to fall asleep. Others wake up at 3 a.m. and don't fall asleep again." Appetite disorders—eating junk food, salt, and sweets—or having no interest in food or eating without enjoyment: those are the two big ones, appetite and sleep disorders. Also digestive problems, headaches, nightmares, fear, anxiety, self-doubt, irritability, frustration, vomiting. Helen is describing life as an employee of a daily newspaper in the Internet age.

Trauma affects people holistically; a whole range of emotions comes to bear. "If you continue to not address the emotions of sadness and frustration and anger," says Helen, "then that energy will go somewhere and attack a part of your body. It can lead to a lowered immune system, colds, flu, and worse. There is so much research being done [on the link] between cancer and lowered immune systems."

I think of my mother, her history of being abused as a child, her rocky first marriage, and her early widowhood. The body works hard to suppress negative emotions because this is America. Americans are supposed to be happy and friendly. We have no time for sadness, anger, or frustration, so the body works very hard to suppress those negative energies. Some people drink more or take drugs—legal or illegal. They start having relationship problems, taking out their anger at work, being short-tempered. Others do self-destructive things.

"A lot of people will fall into depression with grief," Helen says. "The classic definition of depression, if it's not clinical—a chemical imbalance in the blood—if it's situational depression, it's anger and sadness turned inward."

Women have a higher incidence of depression because women are raised to be more ladylike. Cursing, yelling, punching the wall, and kicking the dog are not ladylike. For men, getting into a brawl, dropping a string of f-bombs every five minutes, punching a dashboard, or driving aggressively on the racetrack is more acceptable.

Helen says all my reactions were normal: the shock, the anger, the sadness. "What becomes not normal is if the anger and the sadness and the sense of helplessness stay with you for a long, long time. Then it's not healthy. Then I would say it is really due to what you witnessed or something that goes back to another time in your life. Something that elicited great sadness or trauma and you thought you had come to terms with it and this just opens up old scars and it becomes what we call complicated grief."

Other reactions to grief and trauma are an inability to concentrate, greater difficulty focusing on work, or failure to listen. Someone might have to say something several times. Some people say they think they're becoming senile, but it's typical to have a cognitive change that may last for a while. If it goes beyond three or four months—or certainly the length of a racing season—professional help may be necessary.

Some grieving people lose their faith, turn away completely, and take a break from their spiritual life, not knowing what they believe anymore. Some people turn closer to their faith and find strength in it. Helen summed it up this way. "The thing to remember is that no two people grieve alike. We are all different. Many family rifts occur after a death simply because there's an expectation that everybody should be grieving the same way. It just doesn't happen like that."

My mother made several oil paintings on canvas board during the year before her death, peaceful landscapes of mountains and trees in soft pastel colors. She gave them to family members, one each to Tim, Ritchie, and me. On the anniversary of my mother's death, the first day of summer, I took the painting off the living room wall, removed it from the frame, and took it to an isolated spot in the woods of Avon Mountain. A path ended at an old fallen tree. I'd brought a claw hammer. I set the painting on that altar and crying, tears dripping on the ground, I beat it to pieces. I had thought I was over her death or at least had integrated it into my life. I wasn't. I hadn't. All the years of hating her for divorcing my father, for marrying another man, all the years of fighting with each other—and now she was gone, unreachable. I hated her for dying, and I hated God.

I had saved one of her fashion drawings, storing it safely in a scrapbook. She had drawn it in pencil. It's uncolored, unfinished. This was her life, her unrequited life as a fashion illustrator, an artist, and an independent woman making her way in the world. In it, I can see her hopes and dreams, her optimism. I can hear her laugh as she again repeats her favorite phrase: "You just don't realize." At one time, there were hundreds of drawings in a drawer in the living room desk. I drew on the backs of those illustrations when I was little; she didn't seem to mind. She never said don't do that, these are mine, draw on your own paper. I don't know when she made those drawings because I'd never seen her actually paint one. She drew a fashion model for me once to show the correct proportion and spacing of the body and facial features, but for the most part, I think she worked on her drawings at night after everyone had gone to bed. Those drawings were about her life; the oil painting was about her death.

Every day, I had looked at it hanging there on the wall, mocking my grief. Alone in the woods, I hammered at the painting again and again, take that and that. I hammered until my mother's painting was nothing but pieces the size of postage stamps scattered on the forest floor. Helen Balaban suggests eggs: go into the woods and throw eggs at a tree. She says it's fulfilling, and eggs have the added benefit of being biodegradable. Eggs wouldn't have done it for me, wouldn't have touched my white-hot rage. After I'd destroyed my mother's painting, I left the pieces where they fell. Many times, I went back to that spot. It became her grave, a private place for contemplation.

Shortly after my mother died, I tried not to believe in God, told myself there was no such thing, that it was all bullshit. I took the position, but I never quite believed it. God had been in my life too long. He had found my stolen bike. He liked me just the way I was; a minister had told me so. God was like Mister Rogers. Then I switched from trying to be an unbeliever to being genuinely angry with God.

None of it worked. None of it was convincing.

I sought counseling. My mother had told me before she died that if I ever wanted counseling, I should seek a Christian counselor. I went to a counselor who was also a minister at my church, but I'm not very good in a counseling situation. I tend to want to entertain the counselor. Besides, I'm a man of action. Doing is better than talking, and I knew what I had to do to move on. I had to divorce my wife and end the troubled marriage I had entered too young. It took five years for me to come to terms with my mother's death. By then, I was in the middle of divorce proceedings. I knew what marriage meant, how complicated it could be, what it was like to be married too young, just as my parents had been, to get a divorce, just as my parents had. I *did* realize. I was no better than they were.

After I suffered through my own marital breakup, I was finally able to forgive my mother and father for theirs. My father became my role model in a way. His third wife, Nancy, was the first wife to love him for who he was; she didn't try to change him. She accepted his weaknesses and admired his strengths. I wanted a girl just like the third girl who married dear old dad. They had—and still have—a close relationship that's obvious to anyone who is paying attention. When I married Pat, I deeply missed my mother. They would've gotten along well; I think my mother would've been relieved that I'd met my match.

Helen says that reactions after trauma run the gamut, depending on personality, often depending on how a person has dealt with major losses in the past. Those losses don't have to be deaths. Job changes or situational changes, such as divorce or serious illness, affect reactions to traumatic experiences.

In March of 1980, I was drawing editorial cartoons for the *Dayton Journal Herald*. Editorial cartoonist Dwane Powell at the *News & Observer* in Raleigh, North Carolina, called to tell me I'd won the Pulitzer Prize for editorial cartoons. I asked him how he knew, and he told me his editor was on the committee, that my name was the only name sent to the Pulitzer Prize Board for recommendation. The committee said I was "head and shoulders above the rest." I was floored, but I also knew that nothing was official until the second Monday in April, when the board officially announces the prize. Until then, this was nothing more than a rumor; however, one of the first things I learned in the newspaper business is that rumors spread by journalists are most often true.

I told my editors and family right away. My mother and father, of course, were proud of me. It had taken my mother time to get used to my being an editorial cartoonist. She had wanted me to become an illustrator like Norman Rockwell. I hadn't realized how much until one Christmas, at the height of the Watergate scandal, I bought her a book of Rockwell illustrations. We were looking at it together when she said with a most disappointed tone in her voice, "You could've done this." When I was in high school, I had wanted to be like Norman Rockwell too, but photography had taken over advertising illustrations and magazine covers. Illustration became a dying art form almost overnight. When I got to art school in Chicago, I learned that Haddon Sundblom— the illustrator who'd painted those wonderful Santa Claus illustrations for Coca-Cola—was starving to death on the South Side. I thought if that extraordinarily talented illustrator couldn't make a living, who was I to try? I switched to cartooning. Shortly after that Christmas on the couch with Rockwell, I drew a cartoon of Nixon with his foot in his mouth. My mother loved it, even asking for the original art to hang in the house.

The month between finding out about the Pulitzer and the second Monday in April was the longest month I've ever spent in my life. The rumors were true. Mine had been the only name sent to the board, but the board sent my name back to the committee and told the members to follow the rules; they were to offer three names. The committee refused, saying I was clearly the best cartoonist. My friends at the paper started preparing for the big party at the bar next door. They had bought a jeroboam of champagne, a bottle that came up above my knees. The morning of the announcement, I was too nervous to focus on my cartoon or hang around the newsroom waiting, so I went home. Later in the morning, I went back with my wife. When I walked up to the deputy managing editor, she looked up from her desk and said one word: "Herblock."

I was stunned. How could this be? He hadn't even entered the contest. I turned to my wife and said, "Let's go home." Mike Peters, the editorial cartoonist for the other paper, the *Dayton Daily News*, called and came over to my house with a bottle of Grand Marnier that we killed on the couch, me doing most of the killing.

The story was widely reported. No news organization could write about the 1980 Pulitzers without including the screwing I had gotten from the Pulitzer Board. The next morning, the *Washington Post* and the *New York Times*, among other newspapers, called and asked for my reaction. I was still lying in bed staring at the ceiling. I told them both I felt as though I'd been mugged. My father said, "They're full of bullshit. It's goddam politics." My mother said, "I'm still proud of you, and I love you."

I'd really wanted to nail that prize before she died. I would be immortalized. Encyclopedia Britannica would print my name in every edition until the end of time. In protest, the Association of American Editorial Cartoonists listed me as the winner of the 1979 Pulitzer Prize for editorial cartoons in their annual publication of members' work.

I asked them to print an addendum correction. On Friday, Herblock called and said the same thing had happened to him in 1939, only his newspaper, the *Washington Post*, had taken out ads in the trade magazines, and his parents had flown into to town. He said the Pulitzer Board screws somebody every year and to not take it personally.

Two months later, my mother died. Chuck called to say that she was in the hospital and the end was near. By the time my family and I got to Fort Wayne, she had passed. It was the first time I'd been involved in funeral preparations. I'll never forget the large room almost the size of a gymnasium full of caskets. It looked like a mass funeral.

After the funeral, I went back to Dayton. I'd been struggling with the new editor and the new editorial page editor. They were both born-again Christians and solidly behind the presidential candidacy of Governor Ronald Reagan. I was neither. The editor and I had been hired on the same day five years earlier, and he'd been instructed to make the editorial page more conservative. He started writing columns for the editorial page about accepting Jesus Christ as lord and savior. After three years of bucking the trend, the East Coast liberal Jewish editorial page editor who had hired me left the paper for Washington, D.C., and *U.S. News and World Report*. His replacement was a conservative whose born-again religion seemed to me to be more of a career strategy than a spiritual conviction but stifling to free expression nonetheless. These guys loved cartoons that criticized the Democratic candidate, Jimmy Carter, and his challenger, Ted Kennedy, but became conveniently befuddled when I tried to get anything critical of Reagan published. I knew I'd eventually have to find another paper but planned to stay in Dayton for the time being. It was only two and a half hours from Fort Wayne, and I could visit my mother often while she was sick. I had to hang on. Now that she was gone, I was ready to live as far from Fort Wayne as I could get, outside the Midwest, to finally leave home.

A month after my mother's funeral, the *Journal Herald* sent me to Detroit to cover the Republican convention. I saw and heard for the first time the conservatives, fundamentalists, religious extremists, and not-so-silent majority who were in Governor Reagan's camp. Since the early 1950s, these people had languished at the outer fringe of the Republican Party. They were mainstream media cartoon fodder; the men portrayed as John Birch Society nuts and the women as little old ladies in tennis shoes. Reagan invited them to sit at the table. When I got back to Dayton on Friday, I went right to my office, drew a nasty cartoon about Reagan and his supporters, and took the cartoon to the engraving room without showing it to an editor. It was professional suicide. I knew it, but I didn't care. I don't remember the specifics of the cartoon, but it was designed to piss off both of my bosses. It ran on Saturday. The editor was on vacation, and the editorial page editor was camping with his son. They both called and asked me if I'd gotten editorial approval before running it. I told them no. The editor told me to be in his office in an hour.

Both editors were there when I walked into the room. We sat at a round table, and I fully expected to be fired. I mean, after all, I had hijacked the newspaper. I'd violated the cardinal rule of daily newspapers: nothing goes in the newspaper without editorial approval.

"You know I could fire you," said the editor. I told him that whether he fired me or not, I was giving notice, that I was starting a job search. Suddenly, the tone changed. "Now wait a minute," said the editor. "We can work this out."

I explained that the paper's drift to the right had left me out in the cold, not that I was particularly liberal. I just didn't want to be held down by partisan ideology. I wanted to criticize the Republicans as freely as I had criticized the Democrats over the last four years. I also wanted to be able to change my mind.

I tapped into the old boy network to find my next job. The editorial page editor who had originally hired me told me the *Los Angeles Times* had just bought the *Hartford Courant* and was looking for a full-time editorial cartoonist. I applied, passed the interview, got the job, and moved east, still mourning my mother. The events of that year had not fully settled in. I would be starting over, which I thought would help my troubled marriage. I moved my family into our new home in West Hartford, Connecticut, just after Christmas in 1980.

Events had come so quickly that year that I hadn't given myself time to deal with any of it. Helen Balaban was right; I thought I'd put this all to rest. I hadn't.

The combination of my mother's death and the Pulitzer Prize disappointment had changed my life in ways I hadn't understood until now, until I saw Shane Hammond's wreck. Death is a natural part of life, but my mother's death was about life not living up to my expectations. I thought I had it all figured out. I didn't. I thought I could will events to happen. I couldn't. Most people would say just being nominated for a Pulitzer Prize is an honor. It is, but just being nominated won't get you into the Encyclopedia Britannica.

For a long time, I'd believed in the principles of cognitive therapy; you are who you think you are. I thought I was a failure. Anyone who's ever tried to excel at something faces failure, whether in art, sports, or business. Early in my career, I feared failure every day. Could I come up with a good cartoon that day? Every day? The death of my mother and the Pulitzer debacle seemed to reaffirm my fears. I wasn't able to save my mother, and I lost the Pulitzer to a guy who hadn't even entered the contest. Former man of the house—hah!

It was a long time before I got that shot of adrenaline again, that little thrill behind the breastbone when I drew a particularly inspired cartoon. I wanted that every day. They say racecar drivers are addicted to their own adrenaline. I wanted that addiction too.

Mind Games

Professor John Salamone, a Board of Trustees Distinguished Professor in the Department of Psychology at the University of Connecticut and a race fan, doesn't buy the popular notion of adrenaline addiction. "Someone did some experiments years ago and actually injected people with adrenaline." The researchers found that if they warned their subjects ahead of time about the effects of adrenaline—it increases heart rate, increases blood pressure, and dries out the mouth—people generally didn't have any emotional response to it.

But if the researchers changed the environment, say, showed the subjects a scary movie to prompt a negative response and didn't tell them about the adrenaline or what the effects were going to be, the subjects would feel an intensely negative emotional response. "So the adrenaline itself, on its own, doesn't shape that particular emotion. When the sympathetic division of the autonomic nervous system becomes activated, it too produces chemicals." In other words, as is true of most life experiences, it's about context.

"Most of my studies are about the brain and brain chemistry. A big part of motivation is effort. A lot of people say 'I want to be a racecar driver,' but when they find out what you have to do to become one, they don't do it." Yes, professor, people cursed with an over-developed sense of practicality, not to mention a lifelong devotion to avoiding physical injury.

"Yeah, why do they do it, and a separate question is why do we watch," says the professor. "There are a lot of things that go on in your body when you are exposed to stress and excitement. The interesting thing is that a lot of the things that happen to the body when you're excited in a positive way can happen to your body when it's also a negative experience." A driver can be on a roller-coaster ride, such as a flipping-racecar wreck, and joke about it and walk away or slide into the wall, wind up in the hospital with a concussion and bruised lungs, and fail to enjoy that experience.

The professor suggests an analogy. Let's say I'm walking alone along a trail through the woods when all of a sudden a bear pops up—or Scarface. Most likely, I'd be afraid, but if I were on assignment to shoot video of bears for Animal Planet or to document cases of some degenerate's bullying for *Dateline*, I'd probably also be elated. Afraid, yes—a little—but overall, I'd be excited, mainly because I'd have a film crew and a DEP officer with a tranquilizer gun who could shoot the bear or a bunch of guys like Chet who could kick Scarface's butt.

"I can imagine a combat journalist's having this mix of 'Wow, what a great story, but also, I could've died there,'" says Professor Salamone. Therefore, as far as my television crew and I go, we're not addicted to adrenaline. We're doing something we want and love to do and are paid to do, and we're still getting that rush.

Racecar drivers may be more like someone on assignment for a TV show. A part of their experience is knowing they have to take that curve at high speed to win the race—and the goal is certainly to win the race. "They've done it many times before, and obviously, if they're there now, they have survived, so their experience has told them, hey, you can take this corner at 140 miles an hour." It's about more than adrenaline. Endorphins, the body's homemade morphine, play a role too.

"Stress response can release endorphins, and you can have a reduction in pain." Shelly Perry won her championship season with a broken wrist, and Sean Foster drove the first race of the season with a broken collarbone. "Pain is adaptive," the professor says. "If you walked on nails and didn't have pain, you'd injure yourself. Other times, you want to deaden the pain so you can do what you need to do, and endorphins seem to be involved in that."

Scientists don't know how pleasant feelings arise and if they have to do with the brain, the body, the significance of the event, or all three. The role endorphins play in suppressing fear or contributing to the pleasure process is not clear yet.

Some drivers say that when they get into their racecars, everything else goes away. Driving a racecar at 120 miles an hour brings them into the now. When I drove that open-wheeled Formula Dodge and later, the Late Model, all of my being was focused on that moment, that car, that track. The professor explains: "A lot of this is attentional in nature. What you are doing is so intense that in order to do it, you can't be paying attention to anything else." Maybe it's a little like focusing on a blank piece of paper in a crowded newsroom while people are yelling and joking around and phones are ringing. Of course, in the newsroom, there is little possibility of crashing into a wall and flipping end over end.

The professor also reminds me to consider that racecar drivers—like pilots, cops, emergency room personnel, and fire fighters, to name a few—undergo a great deal of training. Training makes certain thoughts and actions automatic. There are different levels of concentration too. "There may be a time when they say, gee, there was that race when my girlfriend broke up with me the day before and I didn't do so well, so I have to learn to shut that kind of thing out."

Racecar drivers are clearly engaged in thrill-seeking behavior, but it's also true that it is very specific. "Some drivers being interviewed about their street driving are quoted as being very safe drivers. If it all came down to thrill seeking, that would probably work against you in some races. In order to win, you have to make judgments. In fact, sometimes you probably have to suppress the thrill-seeking thing to make the right judgment in order to win, and probably the winning becomes the dominant emotion. If you're in it for competition, the winning, or even doing better than you expected to do, whatever your ranking is, can feel as good as the other."

Drivers, former drivers, and anyone with a lead foot who's driven a racecar around a track say it's the speed that turns them on. "True," the professor says. "I also think it's the mix of speed and control because they could go faster and be uncontrolled, and they would find that to not be such a positive experience." So it's about control and controllability? Salamone explains that there are two dimensions of emotion: valence—is the experience positive or negative?—and arousal, in which adrenaline plays a part. "Some people say there is a third dimension—controllability. These are the kinds of things scientists argue about."

In other words, would a driver feel the same simply being a *passenger* in a racecar? Is part of the thrill of speed the fact the driver is in control? "This is an experiment that hasn't been done," says the professor. "When you're the driver, you are generating the speed. You're creating it, taking that corner, and feeling those forces on your body, but yet, you made it through the curve, and you're feeling great about that."

When I rode with a professional driver in the Late Model driving class, I did it to see how the driver performed, to see whether he drove with two feet or one, and to get a feel for how fast I should be going when I got behind the wheel. It was a thrilling ride, to be sure, but my biggest thrills came later when I was at the wheel, shifting through the gears coming out of the pits, accelerating on the straight, braking into the corner. I didn't go as fast as the professional driver had, but feeling the car respond underneath me made me feel as though I was really accomplishing something, and that was more thrilling than the ride-along.

But what about that addiction thing? I hear it repeatedly from drivers and crewmembers alike. The professor explains. "When I think of the description of addicts and their decision making—these drivers are functioning at a much higher level to make really good judgments. Addicts are well known for not being able to make good judgments.

"Impulsivity is becoming a big area of research—the nature of decisions. One of the implications of it is getting back to this idea of addiction. These drivers don't have the characteristics of addicts. Addicts are known for consistently making very poor decisions, and that's been confirmed in the lab. If you always made impulsive decisions, you probably wouldn't survive as a racecar driver. The training allows the second-by-second decision making. On the one hand, if you're too cautious, you probably won't win. What they have is this narrow window between being overly cautious and too impulsive. One, you die. The other, you don't win." He goes back to racecar drivers' training. "They can see if I do this now, then this will be the result of that, and rather than being cautious, they say, 'Yes, do it. Go.'"

OK, if it's not an addiction, is racing an obsession? "Obsessions are mainly thoughts, the way they are defined psychologically. Addictions are patterns of behavior."

Can these guys be obsessed with racing and not be addicted to it? "Yeah, most people who attain a high level of proficiency at something are obsessed with it. How could you do all that training and not be thinking about it all the time?"

What about racecar drivers' identities? How do they define themselves? "I think profession is a lot of people's identity. It's evident when people are unemployed; they feel like they've lost their identity, their work."

I was thinking aloud about maturity and what role it plays, Modified driver Todd Owen and how he said that he drives differently now that he's in his early 30s. "Different parts of your body mature at different times. The parts of the brain that people think are related to judgment, decision making, waiting, and withholding behavior and deciding later what to do—those parts of the brain are the last to develop, and they take till you're around 30. The Founding Fathers were smart to say you couldn't be president till 35—without having knowledge of neurodevelopment."

Professor Salamone explains that as racecar drivers age, their judgment improves and their experience becomes more complete. At the same time, the body is starting to break down. Vision, reaction time, and physical endurance are not as good. The two curves are going in opposite directions, but drivers who are not at their peak physically can excel because of their superior judgment. Older drivers have a mental library of experience they can call upon in the moment. During a race, everything happens so fast that drivers may not be able to articulate what they know, but they can access it and win. Procedural memory is the key. Procedural memory is about how to do things. It's the difference between knowing a fact and knowing how to perform a task. Procedural memory is not easily accessible verbally. A successful driver has a procedural memory so highly developed that it's a completely different form of knowledge. A racecar driver has different learning systems layered on top of one another to the point where the driver is an extension of the machine. But a human being has to sit on top of that highly developed motor skill with a brain to make the judgments, and the judgment skill has to interpret the automatic part in a split second. The driver's brain is hyper-vigilant, but the body is automatic. The senses are finely tuned, and the possibility of injury or death helps maintain focus. "It's probably a weird state they're in," says Professor Salamone.

I had been in a weird state most of the season, not feeling completely relaxed at any race, afraid I'd see another fatal accident. Other than the horrible beginning, the season was typical with the usual names appearing in victory lane. Every race was exciting to watch, some more so than others. As time stretched on from the first race to the next and the next, I came eventually to accept Shane Hammond's death as part of the show but not quite wholeheartedly. I felt as though I'd lost something: my naiveté, my innocence as a spectator, certainly my ignorance. I had talked to so many drivers who were outwardly bothered neither by Shane's death nor by the possibility of dying on the track. There is only one race left in the season. The image of Shane's mangled car jammed into the Budweiser sign six months ago is still stuck in my mind. Nothing I learn makes it go away.

Believe

The cobalt blue New England sky is cloudless, the long shadows are deep, and the leaves on the tall maples behind the track are turning orange, yellow, and red. On this October day at Waterford Speedbowl, the track's battered red grandstands look almost quaint, like an old country barn. The rusty, bent catch fence seems to stand straighter; the scarred, pitted asphalt track looks blacker in the cool, dry air. This brisk weather holds down the stench in the men's bathroom.

Cars are lining up on the track for an outlaw race, a "race what you brung" event. There are a few Late Models, some Modifieds, a couple of Dare Stocks, and a truck out there, a mishmash of every Saturday-night division at the track.

Pat and I head for the NEMA paddock behind turns one and two. It hasn't rained all week, thank God. When it's wet, the unpaved paddock is ideal for a mud volleyball tournament. Even in dry weather, the dusty gravel gives up a suffocating cloud every time a racecar or a push truck moves. Today, the Pro-4 Modifieds and Legend Cars are jammed in there too. At the tree line, a couple of wrecked school buses—victims of the last school bus demolition derby—sit next to a derelict forklift with a flat tire. Most teams stuck in this back-40 slum bring large sheets of plywood or Astroturf to park their racecars on so they can work. But as ragged as this bullring is for fans and crewmembers, the drivers love it. It has two grooves, low and high, and a driver can win from either one. It's a perfect size for winged Midgets.

Northeast Midget Association racecars are simplicity itself, except when it comes to getting into one or starting it. Getting in requires a svelte agility not many drivers possess. Most Midget drivers are, well, small. The roll cage surrounds the cockpit, and a driver who isn't thin, double-jointed, or Houdini will be a while getting settled.

The seat is snug. Lower bolsters hold the body tightly at the torso, and upper bolsters keep the driver's helmeted head centered. A Midget driver sits straight upright with his or her legs jammed under the seat. To get an idea of what this feels like, sit as erectly as possible on a folding chair, scoot your feet close against the bottom of the legs, and bend both feet up at the ankles until you feel the muscles on your shins bulge. Now imagine heading into turn three at 148 miles an hour, the exhaust pipe screaming in your left ear.

The gas pedal is on the right, down below, hidden from view. The driver has to feel for it. One foot goes on the gas, and above it is another pedal. The driver lifts a foot against that pedal in case the throttle sticks, making a sort of a shoe sandwich. The brake, also hidden from the driver, is a metal bar about the size of a half-inch dowel on the left. Midgets have no starters. The high engine compression ratio of 16:1 or 17:1 in the 300-horsepower motor would require a starter the size of a 10-gallon coffee pot. The power from the motor goes directly from the crankshaft to the drive shaft to the rear end.

To start a Midget, the driver climbs through the jungle gym of the roll cage, fastens the five-point harness, cinches it as tight as it will go, feels for the pedals, and attaches the steering wheel. Then the driver grabs the lever of the positive-lock shifter and pushes it forward to lock in the gears in the rear end. If the car has a T-type shifter cable, the driver pulls the handle and twists it to do the same thing. When the push truck pulls up behind the car, the driver keeps a foot hard on the brake—the tires will skid—until the car is going about 20 miles an hour. There are only two gauges on the dashboard, oil pressure and oil temperature, or, in some cars, oil pressure and water temperature. The driver takes his or her foot off the brake and, when the oil pressure rises, turns on the fuel switch on the left side of the dashboard, flips the ignition switch, and roars way.

Midgets weigh less than 1,000 pounds without the driver, and the lighter the driver, the better. A driver who weighs 30 pounds less than another driver has an acceleration and speed advantage. Weight restrictions vary from year to year, but the basic principle is that the driver should be very light and the racecar motor should be very powerful. An entry-level NEMA Lights Midget is heavier because it has a clutch and a starter. It's powered by a 150-hp motor with a compression ratio of 9:1 or 10:1 and weighs about 1,200 pounds, so it's a little slower. A modern Midget is a vast improvement over the cars of old. Back in the 1930s and '40s, a Midget had a brake lever mounted on the outside left, next to a hand pump. The driver had to pump air into the gas tank to raise the air pressure inside because the motor had no fuel pump. Three hands were needed to drive a Midget in those days, and then, as now, the handling was called "twitchy."

Randy Cabral, 28, says he had a big advantage when he weighed 140 pounds. He's maybe 5 feet 7 at most, has a thick brown goatee but no mustache, and speaks with a decidedly Boston accent. How did he meet Shane Hammond? "My sister was cutting his mother's hair. My sister used to have a picture of me and my father and the racecar at her salon." Shane's mother saw the picture and said her son raced go-karts. Randy had heard of Shane through the kart circuit, so they met at the local kart track that Shane's grandfather Jack Glockner owned and started hanging out together. "We started talking, and he was such an easygoing person, a good all-around kid. It just turned into a good friendship," says Randy. "You couldn't race with someone that was more fun. You'd have a blast any time you were with him. One of my favorite races was at Seekonk. We were battling side-by-side, wheel-to-wheel for ten laps in the feature. I could not pass this kid. He wouldn't let me. I was two years older than him. The caution came out, and that was the only way I could get around him. It was a good feeling because you could always race with Shane. He was clean, and you never had a problem with him."

Randy's father, Glen, drove Midgets in NEMA and raced stock cars for more than two dozen seasons. Randy skipped the usual progression from karts or competitive Quarter Midgets and jumped right into full Midgets. His father, as hard as it is for him to admit, says he was selfish by not bringing his son along in Quarter Midgets. Glen would've had to stop racing for a while, something he wasn't willing to do because he loved it so much. He couldn't miss even one week.

Randy grew up watching his father in Pro 4 Modifieds; then Glen was offered a Midget ride. Says Randy, "I didn't even know what a Midget was, but as soon as I saw it, I fell in love with them as a 10-year-old. I thought they were the best racecars I'd ever seen." He likes that they're over-powered, lightweight, and safe. "It takes a lot more than standing on the throttle to get to the front. You have to have time management. You have to have brains because if you don't, you're running someone over in front of you because you're running so fast and the speed can be so different. You can be so fast in the corners, slow down in the straightaways, and still win the race. You can be fast on the straightaways, slow in the corners, and win. There are so many variables."

Glen decided Randy was ready in 1999 and put the kid in his old Midget. Randy showed promise right away and soon was racing his own car past his father for the lead and the win. Randy was the 1999 NEMA co-rookie of the year.

Randy has an associate's degree in auto mechanics and worked at a Jeep dealership for ten years when he decided to

Randy Cabral at Thompson International Speedway.

enter the school system as a janitor. It was a means to an end. Randy told WickedLocal.net, "I've always had two goals in life. One was to be a good racecar driver, and one was to become a teacher." A former teacher gave him an opportunity, and now he teaches automotive shop at Plymouth South High School in Plymouth, Massachusetts. When he's not racing or teaching, he's working toward a bachelor's degree to fulfill the requirements for a teaching license in Massachusetts. His car owner's wife was an English teacher and tutors him. "Thank God for her. I was nervous, but she helped me pass the tests."

Midget is the only division in the country that has the same specs coast to coast. The Midget is the oldest true short track racecar and runs under the same rules at all tracks, including the motor. "My engine can race from NEMA to USAC to ARDC, any club that's not a sportsman club." The only real difference is winged versus wingless.

"The wing holds it down. Like at Thompson, in my VW-powered car, I never use the brakes. When you drive a wingless car, you have to use a lot more brake." When Randy drives his NEMA racecar in USAC races, he just takes off the wing. Dirt is another matter. "Back in the day, they used to run the same car, just different tires. Now, with technology, the pavement cars are a little different." He can race his winged asphalt Midget—called a combo car—on dirt by shutting off both front brakes or just the right front brake with a control valve so it can help him turn on dirt.

Randy doesn't have a favorite track. "I like them all," he says of the odd tracks, small and tight tracks, and the quarter-milers. "When the cars are handling well, they're the funnest to drive. When they're not handling well, they're the scariest tracks to run." The thing he likes most about Thompson is the speed, but he says you have to respect that speed. "If you don't, it gets you in a quick way. Thompson takes a lot more skill than people like to think." Drafting and aerodynamics are essential at Thompson, unlike at other tracks where Midgets race. "You have to be careful on the speed differences. One car with exactly the same action could be going 20 miles an hour slower. When you're doing 148 and someone else is doing 125, when you come up on that car, you have to make sure you don't run it over." Everything has to be calculated to perfection. At another, shorter track, say Waterford, perfection isn't required. "You can clip a wheel or the wall and think 'I almost crashed there.' You don't have an 'almost' at Thompson." Randy has never crashed at Thompson and admits he's lucky. "I'm nervous there, but I'm praying nothing happens. It's just so fast." In his racing career, he's had four wrecks, the worst at Seekonk when he went end-over-end three times. "It's like a rollercoaster ride as long as you're not hitting anything. Then you realize you're wrecking a $60,000 racecar, and it really starts to bother you."

The thought of dying on the racetrack has crossed his mind. "It's always a distant thought. You try to keep it distant. To me, we have the safest-built racecars. A couple things could be done different with them. For example, you listen to what a lot of people supposedly died from." Every accident is freak, including Shane Hammond's. Nerf bars break and impale drivers, brackets break, seat belts break, the cage breaks, the shark bites. "I guess if it's your time to go, it's your time to go. As far as I'm concerned, a Midget is the safest situation you can have."

Randy didn't see Shane's accident. "I had just passed him, thank God, and I didn't get to see it. That probably would've haunted me. I know it bothers his brother. He saw the whole thing."

Like most winners, Randy gets more than his share of cheating accusations. "A lot of people accuse me of cheating. Just between you and me, I've done nothing different than anyone else has done. I thought I was friends with everybody in the club. When I think someone's doing something, I go right over to them and say, 'Are you doing this?' Show me.

I'm not doing it to be a jerk. If it happened to me, I'd show 'em. I don't have a problem." The rules in NEMA allow a competitor to pay a $100 fee to protest a certain part or component on a car. One time after a race, some drivers wanted to protest Randy's entire car for $100. "I said, 'No, you need to pay $100 for every area on the car you want to check.' They didn't want to do that, and then I asked them why not if you think I'm cheating?"

Cheating claims bothered Randy so much he talked to his father about it. "What are we doing different?" he asked. His father said he and the crew were working together better than anyone else. That's the key to any winning race team.

"I'm a very, very picky driver. I'm so picky, I almost quit racing." When they first started working together, Tim Bertrand, the owner of his car, wasn't listening to Randy. "I'm used to my dad. My dad doesn't have a lot of money, but I would tell him this is what I want, and my dad would figure out a way to build something, fix something, or make that car do what I want it to. He never could make it go faster because he didn't have the money to buy the big-dollar engines, but he would make that car handle. I'm picky. I complain about everything. My dad would say, 'You're so whiny, but at least you give me good feedback.'"

Randy and Tim didn't have that chemistry right away. Tim was used to other drivers, and Randy was used to his dad. If Randy didn't like the way the car was handling, he'd try to get to the front in the safest way. Tim's former drivers hammered their way to the front any way they could. Finally, the two had a big blowup. Tim told Randy to calm down and call him in a couple days. They let the dust settle, and Tim agreed to do whatever Randy wanted him to do, but he wanted more feedback. Ever since then, they've been fast. Says Randy, "Now, me and Tim work like me and my father used to."

Randy admits to being caught cheating once, but it was inadvertent. "I put the wrong tire on the car. It was too wide, 3/4 inches too wide." He didn't know it was a different tire, and it was the biggest race of the season, a tough lesson to learn. The tech inspector knew he wasn't cheating, exactly, but he had to disqualify him, an awkward thing to do. NEMA is a club. They all know one another and help one another with parts, tools, and expertise. They're all friends even when competition gets fierce. "I'm not doing this to get rich," Randy says. "I'm doing this to have fun. When I'm not having fun, I'm going to stay home." Randy is having fun in 2008. He's leading in points and has dedicated his season to Shane.

NEMA newcomer Jeremy Frankoski had just begun to hang around with Randy and Shane. "He was such a nice guy," says Jeremy. "Anything you wanted help with, he'd help. He was a dedicated racer who always did more with less than anybody. It's just a shame to see how it unfolded because he was getting an opportunity with someone who would've helped his career."

Jeremy, 22, has blue eyes, boyish good looks, and the whitest teeth in racing. His Facebook page has plenty of messages from pretty blond girls, one in a bikini. He's driven winged Midgets in NEMA and non-winged in USAC. He describes the difference. "As a driver, I think the winged Midget takes a little more courage to drive well and through the pack as far as sticking it in places you probably shouldn't be putting it in. A non-winged Midget takes more finesse. You're slipping and sliding around on the edge of breaking loose or pushing or abusing your tires." Winged Midgets are faster because they have more corner speed with the wing pressing the car hard to the track, but non-winged Midgets have more prestige around the country. Still, he says, "I think the winged Midgets are more fun to race."

Jeremy is the first driver in his family. His father was a
NASCAR fan, and when Jeremy was 9 years old, he and
his brother Benjamin, a year and a half older, went in together with their dad and bought a kart they saw for sale
at a car show. They stripped it down, painted it, and took
turns racing it. The next season, they built a new kart and
again shared the season. The third season, they each got their
own kart. When they were older, Benjamin loaned Jeremy
the money to step up in racing, and Jeremy paid him back
by working on a farm for $4.75 an hour. Benjamin is still
involved in racing as a crew chief on a few Sprint teams in
New York, Pennsylvania, and Indiana and doing intern work
on a NASCAR truck team. The brothers have a sister and an
older brother who are not involved in racing.

Jeremy likes to get his hands dirty, likes being involved in
preparation during the week, even getting food and drinks
for the crew. He has an engineering degree from Broome
Community College—part of the State University of New
York—in Binghamton. When he's not racing, he works for
a defense contractor that builds circuit boards for the government. The company assisted in the design and manufac-
ture of a device used to jam roadside bomb signals in Iraq.
"When that was implemented, it was very successful and
saved a lot of lives."

Jeremy was also in the race when Shane died. "He was
two cars right behind me. I passed Chris Leonard on turn
two and gained position on him down the backstretch. Then
it was Chris and Shane going into three when they made
contact. Shane collided with Chris." As with most racing accidents, the action is so fast, it's hard to determine who did
what even with instant replay. Wrecks happen in a nanosec-
ond. Some eyewitnesses to Shane's wreck said that Chris's car
slowed suddenly, but Jeremy says there are different thoughts
on the subject. "With our cars at 'T,' the speeds and differ-

ences in motors can really catch up with you. Also, entry points, a lot of people drive it in deeper than other people. The wind can be a major factor. If a gust of wind comes across the track, it can really move your car around and put you in a bad spot with the winged car."

The worst wreck Jeremy has had was at Seekonk when he went sideways into the wall. It knocked him out and put him in the hospital overnight with a severe concussion and a bruised lung. That would be enough for me to seriously consider retirement but not Jeremy—or Eddie Doyle.

My first season in Midgets, I'm in this race at Soldier Field in Chicago. They had a quarter-mile paved oval then. Nice track. Blackie and me had hit the road running a USAC car, and we're winning a lot of races. There was one guy there who had a reputation as a dirty driver. There's always a dirty driver. Every track has one, hell, sometimes two or three. I meet him before the race, and he's making fun of me as a small-town hick in the big city, you know, but he isn't being mean. He's OK, but people there say when he puts on his helmet, he leaves his brains in the toolbox. He's a total jerk on the track, one of these guys who like to take the position whether you give it to him or not.

We're in the first heat race—a heat race, for chrissakes—and I start third, and he's running fourth next to me. He's banging wheels with me even before the green, but I hold my position. The flag drops and in three laps, we're still running three and four when the caution comes out. Coming to the green flag, I give him plenty of room, and in the middle of the backstretch, the sonofabitch turns down on me and hooks my right rear. What the hell—the top four cars qualify for the feature. He didn't need to do that. He's in, but he's being a big shot, showing the small-town guy who's boss. So, anyway, he hooks me, I spin and slam into the wall sideways. I hit my head really hard and spend the rest of the night seeing double. I found out the next day I had a concussion, but I didn't want to give that sonofa-bitch the satisfaction of putting me in the hospital. The wreck damaged the right front, but me and Blackie were able to bend it back and qualify in the consi.

So I start in the last row in the feature and work my way right behind this guy. I'm seeing two of him. By now, I have a headache and I'm feeling like I want to puke. He's running sixth. I get right behind him, and I'm not sure which car is real and which one is my concussion. I squint my eyes, the two cars merge into one, and I hook him back. He spins, hits the turn-two wall, and flips over it into the dark. I think, man, did I do that? The yellow flag comes out, we go around the track twice, and the guy gets out of his car, stands on the wall, and gives me the finger. After the race, the race director comes over to us, and the finger starts bitching and moaning. When he's done, the race director says, "I didn't see anything." Then after a few seconds, he points his finger at me and says, "Don't ever do that again."

A crewmember for one of the Modified tour teams at Thompson told me he had tried many drugs, but racing was the best drug of all, that he must be hooked on adrenaline. I ask Jeremy if he agrees. "I'm hooked on something," he says. "I live for it. When you're in the car, nothing else matters. It's definitely an adrenaline rush. There're very few times you get to Victory Lane. It makes it all worth it. You think one time will be enough, but that's just not the case. You want more, more, and more. A lot of ways, it's like a very addictive drug."

Jeremy is moving to North Carolina after the season and signing with a USAC Ford Focus Midget team next year. These two guys, Randy and Jeremy, are so friendly and posi-tive—in fact, the whole club is like that—that I'm feeling better, I guess, about witnessing Shane's accident. This is what racing is. People die. Shane died doing something he loved, a cliché, sure, but if I'm going to continue to be a race fan, I have to accept that. Amid all these brightly colored cars, I can't help but think of Shane's family at home, dressed in black, shades drawn against the bright sun, mourning their loss. The drivers' meeting is about to start, so Pat and I hang around and listen.

It's Bobby Santos III's birthday. Mike Scrivani, the NEMA president, gives him a small cake with vanilla icing. He lights the candles, and everybody sings "Happy Birthday." Bobby laughs but doesn't pause to make a wish. He doesn't have to. Every driver here has the same wish. After the meeting, Pat and I introduce ourselves to Mike, and I tell him about seeing Shane's wreck in the spring and my reaction to it. "You should talk to Deb." "Who's Deb," I ask. "Shane's mom. She's right over there. Hey, Deb," he yells. I'm stunned. Shane's mother is here? Wait, I'm not ready for this. No, don't come over here. I'm no good with grieving mothers. I don't know what to say. I'm glad Pat's here. She'll know what to say.

A woman and a teen-aged boy walk over. She looks to be somewhere in her 40s, holds a clipboard, has light brown hair, and wears glasses, a NEMA T-shirt, and faded jeans. The boy, as tall as she, with brown hair and a serious expression, wears a black-and-white fire suit. Deb Marvuglio and her son Anthony, Shane's 16-year-old brother. "The g is silent," he says. Pat expresses our condolences.

Deb is smiling, and I ask her how she's doing. "I have good days and bad," she says. Her husband, Tony, isn't at the track today; he comes occasionally, but he's not a race fan. "Just leave me a little money in the checkbook," he tells Deb. Anthony, known as "Bug" to family and friends, drives in NEMA Lites. I don't know—I think if I had two sons and one son had been killed on the track, I'd do whatever I could to keep the other one from driving. I don't come from a racing family, though; I come from a sit on your butt, have a few beers, and root for your favorite driver family. Bug loves being a racecar driver, just as his brother did. "I can get away from everything and just drive." He saw his brother's wreck, the whole thing, the car rising into the air, clipping the top of the concrete wall, flipping into the sign. Then the silence. He has much to get away from.

Doctors diagnosed Shane's brain tumor as pilocytic astrocytoma when he was 15, and he underwent a series of painful, debilitating operations. When he got out of the hospital, his friends and fans in kart racing bought him an $800 state-of-the-art helmet. He lived in pain and took pain management classes the rest of his life. Deb says, "The only time he wasn't in pain was when he was driving that racecar." And there it is—the moment. The moment I understood, the moment my witness was sanctified. Everyone who was there that April day watched Shane Hammond leave this world in his moment of painless bliss. Every driver races for personal reasons. Drivers say it's fun or they like the competition or the thrills, the speed, but it's more than that. It's the soulful expression of life.

***

The Marvuglios' comfortable split-level house is in a wooded subdivision of East Bridgewater, a suburb 30 miles south of Boston. Shane's stepfather, Tony Marvuglio, is the assistant for academic technology at Berklee College of Music. His background is in jazz guitar, computers, and education. "I'm not a let's-go-every-weekend kind of race fan," he says. The smell and the noise give him a headache. "I used to go and videotape, and they'd say every time I taped, they'd lose, so they told me not to tape."

Deb divorced Shane's biological father when Shane was

2 years old. Tony says of Shane, "I knew him since he was a baby. He was like my own kid." Shane's father moved out of state to avoid paying child support, and the boy and his father became estranged after Shane visited him when he was 17. Deb worked two jobs to support her son and put herself through school. Deb and Tony met in a bar in 1982 and married in 1987. "It was the first time I had health insurance," says Deb. She and Shane were very close. Tony says, "She cried when Shane went away, and he cried when she went away. Interesting lifestyle when they were separated. I couldn't console them."

Deb still works two jobs, waiting tables at a country club and at a restaurant but for different reasons—this time, it's to keep racing. She's going to own Bug's NEMA Lite next season, and the costs are staggering, especially in a bad economy. Deb is a second-generation racer. Her father, Jack Glockner, raced stock cars at Thompson and Stafford and encouraged Shane to start racing karts when he was 10. Deb wanted to race when she was young, but her mother wouldn't let her. When she became an adult, she joined the kids in karts. "I took a championship my first year. I loved it. I've always loved speed. I had a motorcycle. My truck came with a radar detector."

"Best money I ever spent," says Tony.

Deb was working with driver Bobby Seymour on starting a Midget driving school in Shane's honor. She says, "I just want to know what the boys experience." Even with two sons in racing, she's never driven a Midget. She asked Shane once if she could just take it around the track. He told her no—there was too much to handle.

When Shane started racing karts, the family—Deb, Shane, her father, her mother, and Bug too, after he was born—made the 250-mile round trip to High Groove Speedway in Winchester, New Hampshire, every week. Bug is a different kind of driver than his brother was. Shane spent hours in the backyard working on his kart. "I was more like, OK, this is fun. Now I want to do something else." Once Bug got into Midgets though, it all changed. "I thought this is sweet." Shane did whatever he could to bring his brother along. Bug shows us a picture of him, Shane, and a Midget car owner. "That's Shane helping me out, saying to the guy, 'If you want me, you take my brother too.'"

Shane's tumor wasn't cancerous, but it was invasive. Pilocytic astrocytoma is a rare juvenile disease that causes tumors to form in the brain and spinal cord. There are certain cells in the brain called astrocytes because of their star-shaped appearance. Something happens to make these cells multiply rapidly, creating tumors. The cause is unknown, and surgery is the only cure if the surgeon can get it all, and that depends on a tumor's location. Shane's started on his brain stem and spread. "It went from his brain stem to his fifth vertebrae, so it deformed his spinal cord. They couldn't take it all out. There was still probably a thumbnail-size tumor left on his spinal cord." Before the operation, the doctors met with Deb and Tony. They wanted to know how to tell this 15-year-old boy that his future was in jeopardy. The brain stem controls most of the senses in the body. No one knew whether Shane would be able to eat, talk, hear, and see. Or race a kart. Deb told the doctors, "I've never lied to this kid, and I'm not going to lie now with his life on the line."

The symptoms started when Shane was in sixth grade, but routine checkups revealed nothing. "I could tell something was wrong," says Deb. "He was lethargic." Shane's tumor wasn't diagnosed until he was a freshman in high school. Deb had taken him to the local hospital. Doctors there said he was dehydrated, that he had a cyst on his brain, and that they would drain it. Then they came back into the waiting room and told Deb an ambulance was waiting outside to take Shane to Children's Hospital. That's when she knew. By the time of the operation, the tumor had stunted the growth of his spinal cord. A normal spinal cord is as thick as a finger; Shane's was like a fishing line.

The tumor had wrapped itself around the spinal cord and affected all his motor functions; he vomited most mornings and had no feeling on his left side. At Children's Hospital, the staff ran a battery of tests that showed Shane's condition was worse than anyone had thought. He was in the hospital several days just to get the swelling down so the doctors could operate. Deb lived there for two weeks.

The surgery took place during the kart off-season in February, but Shane was determined to be ready for the new season in March. He missed only one race. His doctors couldn't explain how his extremities worked—the connection to the spinal cord was so limited. Deb looks at her husband across the kitchen table. "They said, pretty much, we got ourselves a miracle."

Shane's whole left side was spastic, his hips were out of line, he was in constant back pain, and he had no motor skills in his left hand or feeling in the fingers. He called it the "Jerry hand" after Jerry Lewis's goofy comedy. Doctors and therapists worked with him over the years to alleviate the pain. They tried nerve blocks, kinesiology, massage therapy, and acupuncture. Cornell University wanted to put in a morphine pump.

Shane was ill every morning and fought it off. "The only reason he fought it was for racing," says Deb. He woke in pain. He couldn't sleep on his stomach, so if he accidentally rolled over during the night, it would take pain-filled hours in the morning to get him upright. He needed hot packs and cold packs. It was constant. "I was the cheerleader every morning to get him out of bed and get him motivated," says Deb. "We finally found a doctor at Brigham and Women's

Hospital pain clinic who tried Percocet and Oxycontin. They tried everything. Shane was not a good pill person." He didn't like the way he felt on painkillers. He finally used a lidocaine IV drip every month for two and a half years. It eased the pain but never got rid of it. "He honestly never complained," says Deb. "He just was not that person; even in pain, he had a smile."

Shane kept his disability to himself. "He didn't want anybody to know," says Deb. He was tutored at home during his freshman year and entered a new high school as a sophomore. The high school labeled him disabled but didn't do anything special for him, which was fine with him. He rejected the label. Bug didn't know his brother was sick until one day they were driving and went through a tollbooth. Shane was behind the wheel and awkwardly threw his coins into the basket with his right hand.

Shane had to stop racing karts because the g-forces were too much. He had a kart manufacturer sponsor—a factory ride—but the 120 to 125 mph speeds caused his body to move around in the seat too much. That's when he jumped to winged Midgets. A driver is strapped in tight in a Midget seat; there's no sliding anywhere. A broken rib at Oswego was the result of the worst wreck he had in a race, but he got into a fender bender on the street in his own passenger car. Tony laughs when he remembers it. "Yeah, making a right turn."

Physically, Shane looked normal, although his arms were long because the disease had affected his growth. His uniform at the parts department where he worked didn't fit right and neither did his driving suits. Deb persuaded her employer to sponsor a $2,100 custom-made suit to go with the helmet his fans had bought for him.

Deb is all about safety, dedicating her time to improving equipment and track conditions. She devotes time to educating the drivers, asking them pertinent questions. Are they ready to go from a 100-mph track to a 150-mph track such as Thompson? "There's controversy on how Shane died," she says. "A lot of people say the guy in front of him just wasn't ready to go that fast and checked up, and Shane was in full throttle and had nowhere to go." Deb doesn't buy that explanation, saying the owner of the car wouldn't have put a driver he didn't trust in the seat of a $60,000 racecar. "I just don't want it to happen again," she says. To that end, she started the Shane Hammond Believe Foundation, dedicated to safety and driver education. The foundation struck a deal with the manufacturer of an affordable head and neck restraint for drivers. A HANS device costs $1,000, but Deb can supply a safe, comfortable harness for $650. She also has a deal with a company that makes an emergency identification system. The medical bracelets are made of fire-resistant silicone rubber embedded with a computer chip that has all the wearer's medical information. The tracks are another matter.

"Wrecks are a part of racing excitement," says Tony. "But the whole thing is tempered when even as a fan you don't want anyone to lose their life in these things, and that's the difference. There's an opportunity for wrecks on the course, and you don't need the course to cause the wrecks. Things like that have happened in motorsports forever, but it's really the responsibility of the tracks to look at safety and to tell you the truth, I'm surprised. I'm not aware of any organization that goes around and says we're going to shut you down, and that's too bad."

Deb sat down with the executives of NEMA and asked them when they had last looked at safety. Every year, the speeds get faster and new drivers join the club. The execs admitted that they spent more attention on keeping the car counts up than on safety. Every year, NEMA attracts drivers from other divisions who, shall we say, don't get no respect. Deb says, "So now they're going to come over here and run in our playground? Just because you have enough money to own a car and your daddy thinks you should drive doesn't mean you're entitled to jump in the club and drive. I can't tell you how many drivers come in and don't even last a full year. It's harder than it looks, and it requires a lot." The NEMA Lites division has become the feeder series to the main show. The club lets a handful of Lites drivers run in the back of the pack with the full Midgets at the shorter tracks but never at a track like Thompson.

Deb shows us a picture of Shane taken from the back. His shirt is pulled up, and we can see the tattoo of angel wings on his back and the healed scar from his surgery going from the back of his head down his neck to just below his fifth vertebrae. He got angel wings because he always thought he had survived for a larger purpose. He talked about being a motivational speaker one day.

There's a split between Deb's father and the Marvuglio family that has only intensified since Shane's death. I thought back to Helen Balaban's words, that everyone grieves differently. The Marvuglios are building on Shane's legacy, using his name to make other drivers safe. "He lived to race," says Deb. "That was his dream and the only thing that kept him going."

Victory Lap

In August 2007, I couldn't get the Blewett brothers' wreck out of my mind. Modified driver John Blewett III died in a collision with his younger brother, Jimmy, racing for the lead in turn one at Thompson International Speedway. The brother-on-brother irony was overwhelming. I thought it would make a good book, a narrative nonfiction story of their racing family—father, grandfather, sons—all the boys raced. I tried to put it out of my consciousness and just draw editorial cartoons; the presidential election year loomed, but the racing story wouldn't go away. Then one night I dreamed I was interviewing racecar drivers. My wife said I had to write the book.

I planned to start interviews the following spring, at the first race of the season, and pattern the story after Sebastian Junger's *The Perfect Storm*. I even gave my book the working title *The Perfect Wreck*, not disrespectfully, to be sure, but the tragic irony of the accident and even of their last name was too much to ignore. I had a plan. I would get to know the Blewetts and their friends, study tape of the accident, and interview other drivers and crewmembers who had been in the race.

August 5, 2008, I was at Thompson International Speedway in Thompson, Connecticut, for the first race of the season, looking for Jimmy Blewett in the pits. I was way out of my comfort zone, and I felt like a stalker. I found him standing next to his trailer, introduced myself, and gave him a couple of business cards. In my nervous fumbling, I dropped my camera on the pavement and cracked the viewfinder. Jimmy was cordial but didn't say much. Racecar drivers are a singular bunch, and unless you're one of them, you're forever an outsider. That night, I began outlining my book in detail. The next day, April 6, the bottom fell out of my plan.

Racing is the only spectator sport that titillates all five senses. Smell the sweet, high-octane gasoline exhaust, the even sweeter methane exhaust. See the brightly colored racecars with their sponsors' graphics plastered all over the hoods, trunks, wings, and fenders. Hear the loud explosions of 240 to 516 combustion chambers igniting simultaneously, tattooing your eardrums. Feel your chest vibrate. Your beer ripples as the cars rocket by on the front straight; the vibrating metal bleachers tickle your seat. A car spins in turn four, the driver slams on the brakes and hits the wall. First the screech of tires, then the smell of burned rubber, then the taste of dust and Speedy Dry as the safety crew rushes in with the blower to clean up. If that doesn't do it for you, try one of those pulled-pork sandwiches.

Racing is more than a hobby. It's a life, a world, a flat planet where a driver can go over the edge and live to tell about it. And, as 16-year-old driver Dillon Moltz's father told me, "It keeps him off drugs." Racing is the people the drivers know and grew up with, the parents who knew the other drivers' parents. Sean Foster says racing brings people together. A driver doesn't have to be born into it, but it helps.

The dynamic heart of racing is the car. The soul is the

driver. The car is a work of kinetic sculptural automotive art, pulling people in for closer examination, as any art will. Paintings, drawings, racecars. Color, balance, harmony, form, function—it's all there. Maybe I could have been a racecar driver when I was a 20-something young man fresh out of art school, fantasizing in my Oldsmobile F-85 on an Eisenhower Expressway exit ramp in the suburbs of Chicago. I would have had to persuade my young wife to give up her dream of having a house. It was my dream too, more powerful than the dream of racing. With the dream of a house came the dream of a family. Maybe I could have done it when we divorced. I was 40 years old, late to be starting a racecar driving career, but what the hell, other drivers had done it. Instead, I bought a horse. Fact is, the passion to drive is there, but the will to sacrifice for it is not. It's so much easier to fantasize about it on paper and in the grandstands.

I thought I could be a racecar driver until I met real racecar drivers and got to know them. They're laser-focused on driving, and many of them can't talk of anything else. Sure, plowing snow in the off-season, running a scrapyard, or delivering pool water in the summer can be boring jobs. A mechanic's job repairing Mercedes-Benzes at the local dealership is rewarding, but nobody's going to slap you on the back and say, "We won, buddy, thanks to you." These drivers, men and women, are in a club, and once in, they're in for life. And beyond.

***

Since the end of the 2008 season, Deb Marvuglio's Shane Hammond Believe Foundation has become a force in Midget racing. "The foundation has helped a lot of people and saved lives in the process," says Deb. She organized the

Shane Hammond Driving School with Bobby Seymour's First Turn Racing for folks who want to experience driv-

Jack Glockner, Deb Marvuglio and Bug Marvuglio together again at Waterford Speedbowl in 2012.

ing a winged Midget. At the inaugural event, she drove one for the first time. The next season, a new race was added to the NEMA schedule. The Shane Hammond Memorial 37—Shane's car number was 37—was run July 24, 2010, at the Waterford Speedbowl. Russ Stoehr won the full Midget feature, and Randy Cabral won the NEMA Lites feature. Deb says the family still has days of tears or quiet moments, or what they call "Shane days."

Jimmy Blewett parted ways with his sponsors and owners on the Whelen Modified Tour and dropped out of racing for a year to run the family scrap metal business. In 2010, he raced dirt cars at New Egypt Speedway in the Sportsman division, winning his first dirt race and setting a track record shortly after his 30th birthday. He went back on the Whelen Modified Tour in 2012 and in 2013 was racing his new family-owned number 76, the same number and color scheme his late brother, John, had used. At the end of the season, the family announced it were quitting the WMT because of rising expenses.

Renee Dupuis explains: "I can't think of a single cost that hasn't increased. Racing fuel was $9 a gallon in 2008. It was $10.50 a gallon in 2013. We've felt rising prices in all areas, including fuel (both racing and the fuel we use to travel in the haulers), tires, inspection fees, pit passes, licenses, parts, engines, labor costs, hotel rooms, insurance, and mandated safety equipment." A rule change required every racecar to have a new, expensive seat and a quick-change rear end, new equipmnet teams had to buy. The expenses to race one Whelen Modified Tour event now runs about $5,000 to $6,000. "If you combine rising costs," says Renee, "with the fact that purse money has remained the same, or fallen in many cases, the gap only widens."

Renee has run a part-time schedule since 2008. In April of 2011, she became the first woman to compete in NAS-CAR's Whelen Southern Modified Tour at the Hickory Motor Speedway in North Carolina. Throughout the 2012 and 2013 seasons, she competed in the Southern Tour as well as the Whelen Modified Tour in the Northeast. She conducts testing and driving programs to support her racing program and co-hosts a racing themed radio program in Connecticut. Still single, she became a homeowner, buying a house 4 miles from her race shop. Burt Myer, legendary Modified driver and one of the stars from the History Channel racing series *Madhouse*, came up from Bowman Gray Stadium to race the 2010 Icebreaker at Thompson in the Whelen Tour 150-lap feature. Renee beat him by two car lengths.

Todd Owen sold all his racecars except one SK Modified, left his owners, and became an owner/driver with a new number—81—and a new attitude, winning the second-to-last feature race of the 2012 season at Stafford Motor Speedway. In 2013, he added a full-time ride, driving the 17 in the Valenti Modified Racing Series with the Jack Bateman team.

Erica Santos began racing SK Lights in addition to winged Midgets in 2009. She gave up her racing career when she went back to school full-time to become a nurse anesthetist. She and Woody Pitkat are still engaged, and she's hoping to find a ride in 2014. In 2009, they were to race together in a NEMA Midget event at Stafford Motor Speedway when Erica's car had mechanical problems during a heat race. Woody gave Erica his car and worked in her pit crew.

Woody took over the driver's seat for Don King's number 28 NASCAR Whelen Modified Tour car in 2009. Because the Great Recession had taken over the country, Woody had to bring sponsorship money to the team. In honor of the occasion, I designed a cartoon character of a cool cat called "Pit Cat," wearing shades and a driver's suit that looks a lot like Woody's. Woody displays it on the side of the car. At the end of the 2011 season, Don King sold his business and retired from racing, and Woody went to work for a bus company as a mechanic. In 2012, he found a ride with John Lucas Savage's Whelen team. After a devastating wreck at Thompson, Savage retired the operation, and Woody joined the legendary Hillbilly Racing team, where he is today. Woody also left the Hitchcock SK Modified team and joined Gunsmoke Stables. He won the Stafford Motor Speedway championship in SK Modifieds in 2013.

Sean Foster and Christy King broke up. Sean finished a close second in Limited Late Model points at Stafford in 2008. In 2009, he stepped up to SK Modifieds, where he had mixed results, typically finishing in mid-pack. "I would like to consider that a temporary inconvenience," he said. He took over as his own car chief and won his first feature in 2012. He's run competitively ever since. In honor of his

Marvel comic-like nickname, I drew a cartoon character for him, a caped superhero, named "the Grenade." In 2013, Sean started a video series on Facebook and YouTube called *Short Track Racer.*

His brother, Scott Jr., was nearly killed in a snowmobile accident during the off-season in 2009. He suffered extensive internal injuries and endured several painful operations. He still owns his 44 black Pro-Stock Late Model and keeps it on display in the garage, but he retired from driving racecars. Scott competes Monday nights in Senior Champ Kart racing at Stafford Motor Speedway. "I grew up kart racing," he says. He and his wife, Jennifer, divorced in 2011.

In 2012, Ed Flemke Jr. approached Don King about racing again, and Don jumped at the offer. Ed brought a sponsor, and they're running a full-time schedule on the NASCAR Whelen Modified Tour in 2013 and celebrating Ed's 41st year of racing. He says the cars are safer than ever, and the focus now is on certain tracks and unsafe layouts. He used to think, as he laced up his racing shoes, that this might be the last time. He doesn't think like that anymore.

Ted Christopher won the NASCAR Whelen Modified Tour championship for the first time in his career at the end of the 2008 season. He won the 2009 and 2010 championships in SK Modifieds at Stafford Motor Speedway and the 2010 Modified championship at Thompson International Speedway. He bought five of the cars his former sponsor Jimmy Galante owned at an auction ordered by the feds.

Reverend Don Rivers and Reverend Dan Petfield have added three more chaplains and expanded Racing With Jesus Ministries to more tracks and the Modified Racing Series, the STP World of Outlaw Sprint cars, and the World of Outlaw Dirt Late Models. They still minister to the NASCAR Whelen Modified Tour and informally with the Northeast Midget Association. "The future is bigger and brighter," says Reverend Don.

Business is off about 20 percent over 2008 for Billy the Kid, but he says everyone else is in the same boat because of the continuing bad economy in Connecticut. After the 2008 season, Stafford Motor Speedway started a spec motor program for Modifieds and Late Models to save money for drivers and owners. Billy is one of the engine builders involved. "I'm in favor of saving money," he says. His spec motors have won 16 of 20 Late Model races. "I can out-machine the other guy." He calls the spec motor program successful but says most of his business now focuses on built motors for the NASCAR Whelen Modified Tour and the Modified Racing Series. "These guys are millionaires and can afford it."

Mark Arute continues as the COO at Stafford Motor Speedway. Sources tell me that the family settled the ownership issue, and the lawsuit was dropped. Tech directors John Johnson and Jay Shea developed a new tubular metric chassis called the XYZ, and NASCAR accepted it for the whole country. In addition to their duties at Stafford, John and Jay took on expanded responsibilities as technical directors for the North South Shootout at Caraway Speedway in North Carolina.

In 2013, car counts at Thompson International Speedway fell to the point where Don Hoenig and his grandson, Jonathon Hoenig (marketing director), announced ambitious plans to rebuild the speedway's historic 1.7-mile road course and rename the facility Thompson Speedway Motorsports Park. They plan to upgrade the track to modern safety standards, but there still are no plans for a catch fence in the turns around the 5/8-mile oval portion of the new track. They'll be running only one event per month in 2014.

Bear Field Speedway is celebrating its 50th anniversary in 2013 with major renovations, and a new promoter, John Raney, is leasing the track. His goal is to make it more family friendly and get the community involved. The project is not strictly a business decision. His 8-year-old son races karts at the track. Raney has plans to improve the lighting, modernize the grandstands, and build a new scoreboard, and he hired a new general manager and sales and promotion staff.

Ron Stine and Molly Ketzler are still together. She bought him a new racecar, and Ron won a feature with it in 2010, finishing the season third in points. The crew agreed it was better than the old car, but today it's for sale. Ron sat out the 2012 racing season, saying he was burned out, didn't miss the drama, and was tired of spending "tons of money" just to stay competitive. In 2011, he raced a part-time schedule with his old car because he was working so many Saturday nights at the GM plant as it got back to post-bailout production. Ron says he misses driving but not all the work that surrounds it. "It takes a lot more time than just what everyone sees at the track on Saturday."

Randy Cabral won the Northeast Midget Association Championship in 2008 at Thompson International Speedway and dedicated it to Shane. After he picked up the checkered flag, he drove a victory lap, parked his car in turn three, got out of the cockpit, stood on the roll cage, and stretched both arms toward the sky. There were few dry eyes in the stands. He won the championship again in 2009, 2011, and 2012. In 2010, he won the first Shane Hammond Memorial 37 at the Waterford Speedbowl in NEMA Lites and came in third in the full Midget feature. He got his bachelor's degree and is still teaching automotive technology full-time at Plymouth South High School in Plymouth, Massachusetts.

At the end of the 2008 season, Jeremy Frankoski headed south to race Ford Focus Midgets and Late Models. He won the United States Auto Club Carolina Ford Focus championship in 2009 and was named rookie of the year. He raced a Late Model for a team owned by NASCAR Truck and Sprint Cup driver Chad McCumbee and was starting his own ARCA Late Model team, but funding and sponsorship problems ended it. Commuting from North Carolina, he raced a couple of NEMA events in 2011 and took 2012 off to reevaluate his racing career. He started his own business to pay for a ride and hopes to find one for 2014. "I've been sitting out for a year, but I'm going to be racing soon."

Tim and I continue to play golf once a year with our 91-year-old father in Fort Wayne. In 2011, Tim had a hole-in-one—the first I've ever witnessed—on a par 3 at a challenging course in Auburn, Indiana. Ritchie retired from racing in 2013 and is courageously battling pancreatic cancer. With Hoosier stoicism, he says, "I'll either be back at work or dead by spring."

Shane's younger brother, Bug Marvuglio, stepped up to full Midgets in 2011 and won the Shane Hammond memorial race in 2012 after leading every lap. Before that, he won his first NEMA Lites feature race in 2009 wearing Shane's driving gloves. After the race, Bug said, "I thought they needed a ride."

Glossary

brain bar—part of the roll cage behind the driver's seat, also called a Danbury bar. It protects the head.

checker—win

chicane—a sharp S-curve in a straightaway on a racecourse

consi—consolation race

flags—Green flag means go, start the race. Yellow flag means caution: slow down and hold your position. White flag means one lap left in the race. Checkered flag: the race is over. Red flag means stop the race, and black flag means pull into the pits. A black flag with a diagonal white stripe is used for a driver not responding to the black flag. It means scoring has been suspended and a blue flag with a diagonal yellow stripe means a car is about to be lapped by faster cars.

four-banger—four-cylinder engine

groove—the preferred racing line on a racetrack

HANS device—**H**ead **A**nd **N**eck **S**upport device

hot lap—a driver takes the car out on the track and warms it up for a few laps. The yellow flag is out. Then the green flag comes out, and the driver floors it and goes around the track as fast possible. He or she will take several hot laps. The idea is to see what the car needs for the setup for the race and to see how it's handling.

lucky dog—NASCAR's lucky dog rule states that the first driver one lap down automatically gets his or her lap back when the caution flag comes out. Some clarifications and exceptions: if the driver is a lap down because of a NASCAR penalty, he or she is not eligible for the lucky dog pass. Drivers who are a lap down because of mechanical problems are not eligible for the lucky dog until the leaders have lapped at least one car on the track. The driver that causes the caution is not eligible to receive the lucky dog pass during that yellow. The lucky dog rule does not apply during the last ten laps of the race.

mill—motor, engine

NASCAR—National Association for Stock Car Auto Racing

nerf bars—tubular bars attached to the sides of an open-wheeled racecar to help protect the tires

one tire-one compound rule—All racing tires at a particular racetrack must be made by the same manufacturer and of the same materials.

pet, petcock—a small valve that controls the flow of liquid or gas

pinch, as in pinch into the wall—One car sideswipes another, sending it into the wall.

quick-change rear end—a differential that easily allows adjustment of internal gears and ratios

road course—a winding racetrack with left and right turns

second trick—second work shift, as at a factory

short track racing—auto racing on an oval track less than a mile around

still fish, still fishing—basic fishing with a cane pole and bobber

trailer-hitched—two cars racing bumper-to-bumper

Contacts

Shane Hammond Believe Fooundation
164 Anna Drive
East Bridgewater, MA 02333
www.shanehammond.org

Northeast Midget Association (NEMA)
www.nemaracing.com

Racing With Jesus
www.rwjm.com

Stafford Motor Speedway
staffordmotorspeedway.com

Thompson Speedway Motorsports Park
www.thompsonspeedway.com

Waterford Speedbowl
www.speedbowl.com

Lime Rock Park
www.limerock.com

Made in the USA
Charleston, SC
18 July 2014